NOT IN KANSAS ANYMORE

NOT IN KANSAS ANYMORE

✳

Academic Freedom in Palestinian Universities

BY CARY NELSON

ACADEMIC ENGAGEMENT NETWORK
RESEARCH PAPER NO. 1

Preface by Miriam F. Elman

ISBN: 978-1-64921-367-9 (pbk)
ISBN: 978-1-64970-766-6 (casebound)
ISBN: 978-1-63625-050-2 Webpdf (ebook)
ISBN: 978-1-63625-051-9 ePub (ebook)

Published by the Academic Engagement Network (AEN)
Washington, DC . No. I in their Research Paper Series
Distributed by Academic Studies Press

The paper used in this publication meets the minimum requirements of the American National Standard for Information Sciences—Permanence of Paper for Printed Library Materials, ANSI Z39.48-1992.

Manufactured in the United States of America.

Cover photos credits; tornado background: Clint Spencer, istockphoto. com. An-Najah University courtyard: Ameen Rammal, Wikipedia Commons. Color signature credits: 1. Credit: JAFFAR/AFP via Getty Images; 2. Ahmad Talat/NurPhoto via Getty Images; 3. Cam 99/ Stringer via Getty Images; 4. Majdi Fathi/NurPhoto via Getty Images; 5. Issam Rimawi/Anadolu Agency via Getty Images; 6. ABBAS MOMANI/AFP via Getty Images

ABOUT AEN'S RESEARCH PAPER SERIES

The Academic Engagement Network (AEN) is an independently run organization headquartered in Washington D.C. that empowers, educates, and mobilizes faculty and staff on university and college campuses across the United States to oppose efforts to delegitimize Israel; promote campus free expression and academic freedom; support research, education, and robust dialogue about Israel in the academy; and counter antisemitism when it occurs.

AEN's newly launched Research Paper Series provides its members with an opportunity to publish original research that advances AEN's goals and mission. Each academic year, the Research Paper Series will feature three to four papers authored by AEN members in collaboration with AEN's leadership team and distributed widely via online and print formats. The intended audience for the Research Paper Series ranges from academics to practitioners, advanced graduate students, and the informed public. Research Paper authors will be encouraged to revise their work for submission to peer-reviewed journals and academic presses in their respective fields when appropriate. Proposals will be reviewed on a rolling basis by the AEN leadership team.

Successful proposals will be those which address AEN's issues and that have a high potential for subsequent publication. Authors will receive an honorarium upon completion and distribution of their Research Paper. AEN members who are interested in submitting a proposal are invited to do so via our website https://academicengagement.org.

CONTENTS

LIST OF ILLUSTRATIONS

COLOR SIGNATURE (after p. 68)

PREFACE

BY MIRIAM F. ELMAN

In December 2019, a number of violent student demonstrations at Birzeit University near the West Bank city of Ramallah resulted in repeated campus closures, effectively blocking some 14,000 students from attending their classes and completing final exams. The violent rioting was reportedly in response to a new rule set by campus administrators that reasonably aimed to prevent student groups from hosting campus events of a "military nature," including those featuring students wearing masks, carrying weapons, or brandishing "models of missiles." By the time university officials closed the campus to ensure student safety, the protesters had already destroyed the entrance to the campus.[1]

That a major Palestinian university would have to shutter its doors in response to violent student protests might come as a shock to those accustomed to blaming Israel for Palestinian misfortunes. But the reality is that most of the trouble in Palestinian universities has little to do with Israel. Violence perpetrated by campus thugs against Palestinian faculty members has a long and troubling history. University students affiliated with terror groups, with some even serving in student government leadership positions, have for years organized activities on their campuses. Furthermore, this advocacy on behalf of terrorist groups is routinely tolerated by Palestinian campus officials (Caschetta). The result is a learning environment where faculty and students are "afraid to speak their mind . . . Fatah, Hamas, and Islamic Jihad all have

---

1. For an extended discussion of these incidents in Birzeit University see pp. 55.

students available to harass and intimidate faculty who are so named" (Nelson *Israel Denial* 367).

In his masterful 2019 book *Israel Denial: Anti-Zionism, Anti-Semitism, & The Faculty Campaign Against the Jewish State*, Cary Nelson devotes a chapter to documenting these fundamental threats to academic freedom in Palestinian campuses. Nelson assesses how schools in the West Bank and Gaza serve as "incitement and recruitment centers" and the ways in which Palestinian governing authorities routinely fail to "distinguish between valid political expression protected by academic freedom and political expression or political activity that facilitates terrorist recruitment or incitement to violence."

Nelson's book chapter further highlights how, with few exceptions, campus leaders do a disservice to their faculty by refusing to forcefully and unequivocally denounce politically-motivated violence on the campus grounds and by failing to support their faculty. Nelson highlights one example after another of professors being harassed, and sometimes even physically attacked, for voicing unpopular political views. Palestinian factions "police political opinion violently" in their universities, but there is also little evidence that campus administrators do a good job of handling these "deadly threats" to freedom of speech. As Nelson shows, compared to their counterparts on Israeli campuses, Palestinian administrators have an exceptionally poor record of honoring academic freedom.

In this research paper, Nelson expands on the research that he undertook for *Israel Denial*. Drawing on a wide variety of sources, including numerous studies of Palestinian higher education; original interviews with faculty, administrators, and students; and extensive media coverage of events and incidents in Palestinian universities over the past four decades, Nelson aims to correct the "widespread ignorance" about the nature of academic freedom in Palestinian campuses.

This research is important not least because anti-Israel and pro-BDS (Boycott, Divestment, and Sanctions) activists have long focused almost exclusively on the negative impact that Israeli government policies and practices have had in Palestinian universities, "blindly confident" that violent threats to open inquiry and educational rights "come only from Israelis" (Nelson *Israel Denial* 359). In the pages that follow Nelson does not exonerate Israel from all culpability. For example, he recognizes that Israel's counter-terror operations in Palestinian campuses are often more disruptive than they need to be (see pp. 99–100). But Nelson ultimately aims to consider the more serious assaults on academic freedom carried out by Palestinian governing authorities and societal groups. As Nelson notes, by failing to address who and what is actually responsible for the major threats to open inquiry and expression in the West Bank and Gaza, "BDS advocates and other anti-Zionists end up being unable to fully assess the character of academic freedom" on Palestinian campuses.

Not in Kansas Anymore: Academic Freedom in Palestinian Universities offers a sobering assessment of Palestinian campus life. To be sure, as Nelson repeatedly acknowledges, many programs maintain academic rigor and excellence and train their students well.[2] But the universities are also heavily politicized and neither campus free speech nor academic freedom are protected. Hamas, the Popular Front for the Liberation of Palestine (PFLP), and other terrorist organizations attach great importance to student activity and to organizing efforts on campuses. Due to this heavy "incitement environment" campus politics on Palestinian universities bear little resemblance to what Americans routinely experience on their own campuses:

> "One way or another, the campus environment at An-Najah and at other institutions for decades has helped prepare some current students for extreme violent activity. Others leave school to join terror cells and some, in effect, make terrorism their career choice, albeit often for careers cut short by imprisonment or death. It is not just deeply troubling but also definitional that many Palestinian universities have substantial histories of student involvement in terrorism" (p. 86)

What is crystal clear from the evidence Nelson brings to bear is that impressionable Palestinian students can easily escalate from conventional

---

2. This is especially true for STEM programs, where enormous strides have been made in the quality and scope of instruction and important research continues to be done. Recently, for example, contributing to the global scientific community's efforts to combat the coronavirus pandemic, Al-Quds University in east Jerusalem announced that a team of its university engineers and physicians had produced a computerized model of a respirator which could be inexpensively produced (Toameh "Palestinian university").

political advocacy and protest to violent activities that can threaten the campus and the general public. As a result, Nelson argues that despite the quality of many of their academic offerings, West Bank and east Jerusalem schools like An-Najah, Birzeit, and Al-Quds are not really the same kinds of institutions as, say, the University of Kansas: "Allying with a Hamas cell is not the same as joining the College Republicans in Lawrence, Kansas...in the West Bank, we are not in Kansas anymore" (Nelson, 374 and p. 98).[3]

In this research paper and in his earlier work, Nelson documents how Palestinians themselves bear responsibility for the most serious and fundamental threats to academic freedom in Palestinian universities. It's a reality that is largely ignored by the BDS movement which tends to characterize Palestinian campuses as "innocent academic enclaves" repeatedly assaulted by Israeli armed forces.[4] Nelson's research shows this to be an utterly flawed understanding, but it's one that has become increasingly prevalent in anti-Israel discourse. A widely circulated and frequently cited 2018 article in the leftist *Jacobin* magazine is indicative of the now often repeated charge that Israel is perpetrating "scholasticide" and a "siege on higher education in Palestine":

> "The brutality of Israeli occupation isn't limited to wars. It also includes constant assault on Palestinians' access to basic necessities like higher education...it deserves to be documented and organized

---

3. The situation at Gaza's Islamic University is even more comprised. While Hamas doesn't run the campus, the overlap between the terrorist organization and the school is almost seamless. As a result, it's simply ludicrous to claim that any meaningful academic freedom exists there.

4. For example, in recent years, the *Middle East Studies Association* (MESA), via its *Committee on Academic Freedom* (CAF), has written numerous "advocacy letters" addressed to Israeli government officials demanding an end to alleged arbitrary arrests and IDF incursions into Palestinian universities. In these many missives, there is little indication that MESA/CAF is aware of the long history of terrorist recruiting or pro-terrorist activity in Palestinian campuses. See, for example, MESA/CAF's March 13, 2018 and January 22, 2019 letters to PM Netanyahu and other Israeli government officials condemning the IDF's arrest of Omar al-Kiswani and Yehya Rabie, both Presidents of Birzeit University's Student Council. Nelson flags al-Kiswani's arrest and questions MESA/CAF's approach on pp. 96–98.

against for what it is: a slow, sadistic crushing of learning, and a stifling of the life opportunities it provides." (Riemer)

Today, any pro-BDS petition or resolution fielded on an American campus or at a US professional association is likely to include wild allegations about Israel denying academic freedom to Palestinian faculty and students—and to foreigners who are supposedly being denied access to teach and study in Israel and on Palestinian campuses. Accusations that Israel wantonly and deliberately discriminates against Palestinian and foreign national academics and students now also feature prominently in pro-BDS messaging used to justify the boycott of Israeli academic institutions.

Consider, for example, the pro-BDS resolutions that were up for discussion in the summer of 2019 at the annual meetings of the *American Political Science Association* (APSA) and the *Society for the Study of Social Problems* (SSSP). At APSA, a resolution to boycott Israeli academia was proposed by some members of one of its organized sections, *Foundations of Political Theory* (JNS "Resolution to boycott"). The resolution laudably advocated for the academic rights of Palestinian students and scholars in Palestinian universities yet maintained that Israel's "colonization of Palestine" is to blame for "consistently and brutally" denying academic freedom to Palestinians. Like the APSA "Academic Boycott Resolution," the SSSP resolution urged that the association "refrain from participation in any form of academic and cultural cooperation or joint projects" with Israeli academic institutions, and recommended that SSSP members pressure their own universities and colleges to "suspend all ties with Israeli universities, including collaborative projects, study abroad, funding and exchanges." In this case too, the call for academic boycott was justified on the grounds that Israel is "limiting," "inhibiting," and "routinely violating" the academic freedom of Palestinian scholars and students, with such allegations featuring throughout the document.[5]

---

5. For more on the deliberations over the pro-BDS resolution at APSA see JNS, "Resolution," and Gerstman, "Pro-Israel Scholars Counter Move." For more on last year's effort at the SSSP to pass a resolution calling for the boycott of Israeli academic institutions, see Gerstman, "Opposition Grows to Pro-BDS Resolution," and Gerstman, "Major US Academic Association Votes Down Resolution." Although the resolution was voted down at the prior annual

Another example surfaced at the annual *American Historical Association* (AHA) this past winter. While not advocating for a wholesale academic boycott of Israel, two pro-BDS resolutions fielded at the AHA's annual meeting in January 2020 also rested on allegations that Israel targets Palestinian academic freedom and Palestinian institutions of higher learning. Both of the AHA resolutions cast Israel as solely responsible for restrictions on academic freedom in Palestinian universities with this charge featuring prominently in their texts. Several documents aimed at countering the resolutions were prepared by the *Alliance for Academic Freedom.* They maintained that while purported to protect educational access and academic freedom in Israel, the West Bank and Gaza, the pro-BDS resolutions were one-sided against Israel. In particular, the AAF noted that they failed to consider the far worse track records of many other countries, including other democracies like the US and the United Kingdom, on issues related to access to education; unfairly criticized Israel's policies by omitting the overall security context; and condemned Israel without discussing how Hamas, the Palestinian Authority, Egypt, and Jordan limit Palestinian educational opportunities and violate academic freedom.[6]

Recent anti-Israel activism at Columbia University in opposition to an educational partnership and dual degree program forged between the NYC campus and Tel Aviv University (TAU) serves as another case in point (Azad Essa). The program was announced with a Fall 2020 starting date. A petition prepared by the campus *Students for Justice in Palestine* chapter and Columbia/Barnard *Jewish Voice for Peace,* called for the suspension of an announced dual-degree program between Columbia's School of General Studies (GS) and TAU on the grounds that, if Columbia went forward with the program, then it would be at

---

meeting, and considerable opposition to academic boycotts was voiced, pro-BDS scholars in the SSSP are at the time of this writing once again proposing a virtually identical resolution for consideration at the Society's Annual Business Meeting scheduled for August 7, 2020. This is despite the fact that the COVID-19 pandemic has necessitated a truncated deliberation period for all proposed resolutions as well as an online voting mechanism.

6. For more on the effort to defeat the AHA resolutions denouncing Israel, see Herf, "Historians Defeat Resolutions Denouncing Israel," and Marks, "A Model Response to BDS."

risk for violating its own non-discrimination policy and Title VI of the
Higher Education Act because Columbia students would be prevented
from attending the GS-TAU program "on the basis of their race and/or
national origin." In particular, the petition referenced the March 2017
amended Entry into Israel Law, which the petitioners claimed "effectively criminalizes mainstream and accepted forms of humanitarian
advocacy" and "refuses to recognize the rights of political expression
granted to students by the United States Constitution."

But this recently-launched dual degree program will hardly put
the university's academic integrity at risk by "excluding a substantial
portion of prospective students," as the petitioners claim. In fact, the
concern that this new educational collaboration will be inaccessible to
Arab or Muslim students enrolled at Columbia, or to pro-BDS student
activists studying there, is grossly overblown and relies on a misunder-
standing of Israel's amended entry law. Here, Nelson's assessment is
helpful (see pp. 129–136). While he finds the amendment to the entry
law "misguided," he points out that in the years since it went into effect
only 16 foreign nationals have been barred from entry into Israel on
BDS-related criteria, and of those only one was an academic (ironically,
Katherine Franke, a faculty member at Columbia).[7]

Nelson notes that neither U.S. faculty, much less U.S.-based students, are routinely denied educational opportunities in Israel. This
is because the 2017 amended entry law applies only to key foreign-
national activists who serve in "senior or significant positions/roles" in
organizations that actively and continuously promote anti-Israel delegitimization and boycotts. Furthermore, according to the government's
criteria for barring boycott activists from entering Israel, "the fact that
an anti-Israel or pro-Palestinian organization has a critical agenda vis-
à-vis a policy by the Israeli government" does not constitute grounds
for a denial of entry. Nelson's thoughtful discussion of foreign faculty
and student travel to Israel and the West Bank (pp. 129–136) offers

---

7. Nelson (pp. 132–133) notes that Franke was barred from Israel in 2018
because of her prominent leadership position in the virulently anti-Israel and
pro-BDS organization *Jewish Voice for Peace* (JVP). For more on the role that
JVP plays in the BDS movement, see Bennett , "JVP's Anti-Semitic Obsession
with Jewish Power," and Elman, "Jewish Voice for Peace."

important context that is typically either ignored or dismissed out of hand by the BDS movement, including legitimate security concerns.[8]

Taken as a whole, this research paper is an important addition to a growing body of work that evaluates Palestinian academia and the *Academic Engagement Network* is proud to feature it as the inaugural paper in our recently launched *AEN Research Paper Series*. Beyond offering a comprehensive and detailed overview of campus life in the West Bank and Gaza, *Not in Kansas Anymore: Academic Freedom in Palestinian Universities* persuasively challenges a now central BDS complaint, namely that Israel is responsible for violating the academic freedom of Palestinians and for the "silencing of Palestinian contributions to knowledge."

A key flaw of BDS is that it turns a complex and intractable conflict into a caricature which singles out one side for blame and establishes a false binary of oppressor vs. oppressed. Regrettably, as Nelson meticulously documents in this research paper, such biases and distortions carry over into BDS characterizations of Palestinian academia where open inquiry is severely restricted by harassment and even violence perpetrated by activists and groups linked to terrorist organizations, feckless administrators who tolerate this terror-linked activity, and the heavy-handed policies of Palestinian government officials which severely chills free expression. Nelson puts it well: "Palestinian-on-Palestinian coercion, intimidation, and violence are part of the daily routine of university life" (p. 21). It is at once irresponsible and tragic that pro-BDS activists, who profess to care deeply about the welfare and well-being of Palestinians, continue to ignore these substantial threats to academic freedom that originate from Palestinian governing authorities and societal groups themselves.

---

8. To his credit, Nelson acknowledges the current difficulties that foreign academics face in traveling to the West Bank to teach and study. But Nelson rejects the assertion that foreign nationals seeking to travel to Palestinian universities are "arbitrarily" denied entry. He also rightly points out that when the requirements for obtaining visas are circumvented, international academics should not be surprised to find their subsequent applications denied.

ACKNOWLEDGEMENTS

Not in Kansas Anymore is substantially revised and expanded from chapter ten in my 2019 book *Israel Denial: Anti-Zionism, Antisemitism, & The Faculty Campaign Against the Jewish State*, jointly published by AEN and Indiana University Press. I owe my first thanks to Miriam Elman for suggesting I take on this project and for tracking down several important facts cited here. My thanks as well to Spencer Kent, Raeefa Shams, Naomi Grant, Ken Stern, Paula A. Treichler, Kenneth Waltzer, and others for suggestions they offered about drafts of this essay and to Michael Atkins for helping with publication. Thanks to Seth Ward and Russell Berman for translations from the Arabic. My particular thanks to Raeefa for her unusually detailed comments.

In the course of researching this longer version—it has grown from 11,000 to 50,000 words—I decided I needed to address several topics beyond the scope of the original essay. I also realized that it really did not work to limit my account of the history of Palestinian higher education to representative examples, as I had before. If the reader was to fully comprehend and accept the reality of a higher education system saturated with politics, it would be necessary to give more comprehensive accounts of at least major indicative practices and events. That included telling the story of university student involvement in lethal violence more fully than others had done before.

My title of course borrows a phrase from Dorothy's famous remark to her dog in *The Wizard of Oz*: "Toto, I've a feeling we're not in Kansas anymore."

NOT IN KANSAS
ANYMORE

✳

Academic Freedom
in Palestinian Universities

INTRODUCTION

> In Palestine limits on academic freedom are brutally enforced.
> —Steven Salaita, *Inter/Nationalism*, 45[9]

Let us begin with Professor Sari Nusseibeh's riveting account of what transpired after he taught a philosophy class at Birzeit University on the West Bank on September 21, 1987:

> Most of the day I am at home preparing for my Monday morning lecture at nine o'clock. The theme was to be John Locke, liberalism,

---

9. Steven Salaita is one of the most fiercely anti-Zionist writers in the US. In 2014 he famously tweeted "Zionists: transforming 'anti-Semitism' from something horrible into something honorable since 1948," one of a series of public statements that convinced the University of Illinois Board of Trustees not to sign his faculty employment contract. See the chapter on Salaita in my *Israel Denial* for a very full analysis of his publications and employment problems. This essay is devoted to demonstrating that, contrary to Salaita, it is Palestinians themselves, not Israelis, who compromise academic freedom.

and tolerance. Typically three hundred students would show up for such a lecture.

On Monday morning I arrived in the lecture hall, took my place at the podium, and immediately launched into my thoughts on Locke . . . . The lecture finished and most of the students filed out of the hall, while a few stayed behind to ask me some questions. A couple of colleagues in the department also lagged behind, and as I slowly moved toward the door surrounded by a small huddle of pupils, one female colleague informed me in a rather shaky voice that a pack of masked men with clubs were outside in the hallway stalking a "traitor." It was only when I reached the door that it occurred to me that I was the "traitor."

Five kaffiah-wearing attackers came right at me. As they attacked me with fists, clubs, a broken bottle, and penknives, I tore myself away from them and ran into an open elevator. A female student rushed in with me, taking some of the blows. Frantically pressing the buttons, she realized that the elevator wasn't working, and rushed out again. One of the attackers clubbed her as she ran away. Now, as I stood by myself with my back to the wall of the elevator, I felt at least protected from behind; they could only get at me from the front. I did my best to defend myself using arms and feet, but knew it was like swimming against a strong current. If I stayed I'd quickly succumb to exhaustion, and the five assailants would finish me off. For some reason, the American saying "sticks and stones may break my bones" shot through my mind.

With a rush of adrenaline, I threw my whole body at the hooded thugs, caused a breach as in a rugby match, and dashed pell-mell through the hallway and down the staircase, with the attackers in hot pursuit. It was only upon reaching the ground floor, which was crowded with students, that they fled. By now blood was oozing from my forehead and wrists, and my heart was pounding loud enough to pop my eardrums.

The colleagues who had been kept away with knives ran up to me. One was the husband of the woman who had warned me in the lecture hall. He offered to drive me straight to hospital. A friend from my Café Troubadour days put my good arm—the other was broken—around his shoulder, and helped me to the parking lot.

Lucy [Nusseibeh's wife] had just finished teaching when it all began. She heard the hubbub and asked someone what was happening, and got a shrugged response, "Just a traitor." When she found out what had happened and to whom, she rushed to the hospital, driven by one of my friends.

In the hospital in Ramallah where I was first taken, the surgeon stitched up the gaping gash above my eyelid. My broken arm was set at the French Hospital in Jerusalem . . . . The public reaction was mute, to put it mildly . . . . The university administration came out with a halfhearted and very general statement denouncing political violence on campus. The union said nothing; only its Fatah faction, led by another stalwart, Sameer Shehadeh, came out against the attack. The Fatah student organization couldn't figure out what to do, so they put out two statements, one in my defense and the other hinting that I had a good beating coming to me.

—Sari Nusseibeh, *Once Upon A Country: A Palestinian Life*, 260-61

Nusseibeh was a philosophy professor at Birzeit from 1978 to 1991 after studying at Oxford and receiving a doctorate in Islamic Philosophy from Harvard. He would later become President of Al-Quds University in east Jerusalem, serving there from 1995–2014.[10] The Nusseibeh family's Jerusalem history can be traced back over a thousand years. For a time Nusseibeh taught classes in Islamic philosophy at Hebrew University of Jerusalem.

At Birzeit, Nusseibeh would before long learn that, of those masked men who attacked and were willing to kill him, "All were students at Birzeit, and a couple I knew quite well" (263). The crime for which he was punished that day was having held several meetings with Israelis to discuss possible peace proposals. PLO chair Yasser Arafat had been kept apprised of the developing conversation, and his staff had confirmed

---

10. Al-Quds was actually founded as a 1984 union of four colleges—the Religious Studies College of Beit-Hanina, the Islamic Archeology Center in Shekh-Jarrah, the Hind al-Husayni College for Women, and the Science and Technology campuses in al-Bura and Abu-Dis.

that Nusseibeh should proceed. No matter. Fatah itself was divided between militant and political factions. Indeed, a Fatah leaflet attacking Nusseibeh had been distributed in Jerusalem (262).

Although the Birzeit faculty union chose not to support Nusseibeh, he had, ironically, been its first chair. Reflecting on his selection years later, he was both self-effacing and bemused: "Since I was one of the few faculty members not belonging to a faction, process of elimination had landed them at my door" (185). Nusseibeh makes an important point. Once the First Intifada was under way, it was not just students who aligned themselves with mutually hostile political factions. The faculty were equally divided and politically committed. That process was already under way before then, but it was completed in the 1980s. As Nusseibeh reports, the consequences of "the bare-knuckle workings of politics at the university" could be chilling:

> Soon after I arrived I was dragooned into a heresy trial. A professor, the American-educated political scientist Nafez Nazzal, had transgressed the national ethos that considered Sadat a traitor and the autonomy deal he had agreed to at Camp David a sellout by meeting with American officials at the American consulate to discuss the Camp David Accords. A faculty meeting was convened to take him to task for it. As I entered the hall, I saw Nafez standing on the stage, microphone in hand, absorbing rhetorical blows from all sides. He couldn't get a word in, so loud was the inquisitional clamor . . . . Professor Nafez, isolated and harried, served as a warning. (161)

As Antony Thrall Sullivan, a scholar who published original archival research about French colonialism in Algeria before turning his research to the occupied territories, reports about the impact of academic freedom in *Palestinian Universities Under Occupation,* following a conversation with Birzeit political scientist Emile Sahliyeh, "From within, Palestinian political cleavages inhibit totally free expression. A supporter of Jordanian-Palestinian federation, for example, would likely be denounced by others at Birzeit as a traitor" (29).[11] He adds

11. Sullivan worked from 1970-2000 at the Earhart Foundation in Ann Arbor, Michigan. He taught at the International College in Beirut and, since 1988, has held an appointment as associate at the Center for Middle Eastern and

a comment from a senior An-Najah University administrator: "The 'political limitations' on intellectual freedom issue from 'student groups (primarily) and some faculty members'" (51). That has been the case throughout the history of Palestinian higher education. As former Al-Quds faculty member Mohammed Dajani, profiled below, observed about Palestinians generally in 2020, "they avoid expressing moderate views for fear they will be accused of being traitors or collaborators" (Nurding).

The pattern of Palestinian violence against Palestinian faculty members has a long history. Repeated incidents took place, for example, during the factional conflicts of the early 1980s. Palestinian author and politician Ziad Abu-Amr cites a particularly chilling example:

> Najah University in Nablus was the site for other confrontations and clashes. In the last part of 1981, the university was the scene of violent clashes between Muslim Brotherhood and pro-PLO students. The conflict had erupted as a result of the nationalist students' demand to restore four lecturers to their positions after the university administration had dismissed them. On January 9, 1982, more than twenty-five persons were injured at a similar clash at the same university over the same issue. During this clash, Muhammad Hassan Sawalha, a lecturer at the university known for his sympathy for the nationalists, was thrown from the third floor of a university building and suffered serious injuries. (45)

North African Studies at the University of Michigan. When drawing on earlier critiques of or generalizations about Palestinian higher education, I cite only observations that remain valid today. For example, lists of available majors and academic specializations and enrollment statistics from earlier decades are no longer valid. University web sites are a better source for that information. It is also important to be aware that there is overheated rhetoric and overstated claims from all political perspectives regarding the conflict. Some concerns have arisen only recently. Thus Awajneh et al report a high degree of Palestinian faculty awareness that they are embedded in a worldwide knowledge economy, but only moderate ability to act on the basis of that awareness. They point out that Palestinian faculty "need more training in working as groups and as researchers in research groups in various specializations" (87) and need to promote "understanding world culture and its terms, and dealing with it positively without intolerance or bias" (81).

It is important to recognize at the outset that, unlike some of the knife and car ramming attacks carried out against Israelis since 2015, the violent actions detailed in what follows are not typically isolated or impulsive copycat acts by individuals, though even individual action that seems impulsive is usually inspired by public endorsement of anti-Jewish violence. Almost all the violence described below required group planning, coordination, and execution. These are not the lone wolf actions of troubled individuals that we have occasionally seen in US secondary and post-secondary educational institutions. Moreover, far from being condemned as horrific and unacceptable, they are regularly celebrated (Figs. 3, 4, 7, 8, 9, 10, 11, 12, 13). This is interpersonal violence carried out with wide social support, both on campus and in the community. "Terror attacks and plots do not take place in isolation. They are fostered by an online environment of hate, bigotry and extremist content" (Community Security Trust 7). All of this creates a culture of campus and campus-related violence that has been sustained for forty years and will be very resistant to change. The absence of productive, nonviolent student and faculty activism make Palestinian campuses highly unlikely sites for the promotion of reconciliation, a viable peace process, or the development of a two-state solution to the conflict.

Predictably, some faculty critics of the first version of this essay—which gave a preliminary account of the way Palestinian factions police political opinion violently and undermine academic freedom in their own universities—declared that the essay was clearly racist. Graduate students who were part of the pro-BDS (Boycott, Divestment, and Sanctions) coalition in the Modern Language Association (MLA), the professional association representing English and Foreign Language teachers, echoed the two accusations at the organization's annual meeting in January 2016. The accusation of racism was designed to discredit the essay in advance of anyone reading it, to cut off discussion of its substance and render it illegitimate.

Debates about the status of academic freedom in Israel, Gaza, and the West Bank have for years focused almost exclusively on claims about the negative impact particular Israeli government and Israeli Defense Forces (IDF) policies and practices have had on Palestinian students and faculty. While the BDS movement levels accusations against Israel and promotes boycott and divestment resolutions directed against it, the broader character of academic freedom on Palestinian campuses is largely ignored. There is little evidence that students and faculty in the West know what the major threats to academic freedom in Gaza and the West Bank are, let alone who is responsible for carrying them out.

This paper aims to correct that widespread ignorance. It will cover two generations of what has so far been minimally reported Palestinian violence, gather that history and its many incidents together for the first time, and conclude with a section analyzing the most frequent complaint about Israel's impact on Palestinian academic freedom—that Israel restricts foreign faculty travel to teach at Palestinian universities in the West Bank.

By ruling out of consideration all assaults on academic freedom carried out by Palestinians themselves, BDS advocates and other anti-Zionists end up being unable to fully assess the character of academic freedom in the West Bank and Gaza. Based largely on Israeli-imposed travel barriers and campus closures, Berkeley faculty member Judith Butler in her 2006 piece "Israel/Palestine and the paradoxes of academic freedom" endorses the claim "that there is no effective academic freedom for Palestinian students in the occupied territories." She then asserts that, among other criteria, academic freedom requires "the right to be free from violent threats." Like former faculty member Steven Salaita in the initial epigraph for this essay, Butler is blindly confident that West Bank threats of violence come only from Israelis. But I open this essay with accounts of violent assaults directed and carried out against several faculty members by Palestinian factions. These are part of efforts by various Palestinian political factions to constrain speech, curtail academic freedom, and punish those who oppose their beliefs. Some who are unwavering in their hostility to Israel accuse it of "a constant assault on Palestinians' access to basic necessities like higher education," "a slow, sadistic crushing of learning, and a stifling of the opportunities it provides" (Riemer). Yet the deadly threats to freedom of speech come from Palestinians, not Israelis.

If the Palestinian students who attacked Nusseibeh were, in one sense, victims, denied citizenship rights in the occupied territory of the West Bank, in another important sense they had obvious political agency. They were capable of policing the campus and of carrying out a violent attack on a faculty member, punishing him for the "crime" of collaboration. They did so even though Nusseibeh sought an Israeli withdrawal to its pre-1967 borders, a position on the conflict that itself apparently warranted the accusation of collaboration, since it accepted the existence of a Jewish state within Israel's pre-1967 borders. In one part of their lives the students were victims; in another, they were perpetrators. Structurally similar but different dual identities can obtain for Palestinian faculty as well. After a 2010 visit to West Bank universities, Amy Kaplan noted that the Palestinians she met "did not only identify themselves as victims but also as cosmopolitan intellectuals struggling to build a civil society in which the university plays a central role."

Faculty members in the humanities are well aware that people can hold multiple (even contradictory) identities at the same time. Yet many are unwilling to apply that knowledge to their anti-Zionist politics. Responding to the much shorter version of this essay published in *Telos* in 2015, BDS-allied faculty members at the January 2016 annual MLA meeting castigated me for "blaming the victim." Palestinians in their view were pure victims, incapable of any action or identity beyond embodying their victimhood. In the Manichean psychology promoted by the BDS movement, there are victims on one side of the conflict, perpetrators on the other. On each side, all the members are depicted as identical and interchangeable. In what follows, I will continue to cite research by Palestinians criticizing their own institutions. Are they blaming the victim?

It is crucial, however, to recognize that Palestinian students and faculty are *intersectional victims*—victims simultaneously of the unjust elements of the occupation and of their own recurrent traditions of celebrating political violence among and by Palestinians. As a category employed in an open-minded manner, intersectionality can capture the interaction of opposing political forces. Much of the international higher education and governmental community has been in fundamental denial about the doubly victimized psychological, political, and institutional status of Palestinian higher education. As this essay will show, Palestinian-on-Palestinian coercion, intimidation, and violence are part of the daily routine of university life. By gathering an indicative quantity of the evidence behind that claim in one place for the first time, this essay issues a challenge to confront reality to all those interested in the Israeli-Palestinian conflict. Yet I have no illusion that the worldwide anti-Zionist community will even process the factual evidence presented here. The anti-Zionist BDS movement will remain in obdurate denial. But others will hopefully learn from what is recounted here and ask how the character of our conversations about Palestinian universities and about the Israeli/Palestinian conflict should change as a consequence.

To document such incidents, this essay draws on a review of relevant news reports and scholarly essays, as well as on numerous interviews I conducted in the area from 2014 to 2019. Using many examples, I aim to promote a wider understanding of the realities on the ground in the Palestinian territories. In order to capture the character and range of news coverage of the issue, I cite stories from numerous different sources and countries and by reporters and groups with very different political perspectives. I draw on news stories, editorials, NGO and governmental reports, and academic research. This wide variety of national and political citations creates a high degree of consensus around this project's key claims, even though many writers may be unaware of (or even resistant to) the factual and analytical agreement to which they have contributed.

This consensus about the facts—sometimes unwitting, sometimes directly argued—includes a considerable record documenting the political, cultural, educational, and psychological impact of violence and the celebration of violence on Palestinian campuses. Thus, a journalist can write about a single violent event and treat it as a unique event. But when scores of journalists do so, they have contributed toward the case that the culture of violence is pervasive and recurring. Hamas- and Fatah- identified writers often tend to document only their opponents' acts of violence and intimidation. Part of what I have done here is to cite both sets of accounts.

My analysis covers individuals, issues, and institutions. It opens here and in the next section with detailed portraits of three Palestinian faculty members, each of them unique but each facing responses and consequences that are instructive and often representative. Beyond these faculty members, whose stories have been widely covered in the press, in a few cases I have withheld the names of people interviewed to protect their safety. That includes the names of Palestinian students with whom I spent some hours on multiple occasions.

Academic freedom is (or should be) higher education's central guiding principle worldwide, though there are countries where its invocation really only serves as a public relations cover for repression. If faculty and students cannot express controversial positions without fear of reprisal—as faculty and students under Hamas, the Palestinian Authority, and Islamic Jihad surveillance clearly cannot do—then academic freedom is fatally flawed, and the colleges and universities they work in cannot be devoted to the search for the truth. The gold standard for practice is "to ensure that scholars and students can peacefully think, question, and share ideas without retribution" (Scholars at Risk, *Free to Think 2019*, 19). A few years ago, Palestinian activist Bassem Eid told me the story of a faculty member who ran afoul of the Palestinian authorities simply because he assigned his students to write a paragraph commenting on the PA. The absence of any freedom students had to be critical of the authorities made the assignment unacceptable. That gives one indication of how thoroughly Palestinian surveillance penetrates West Bank campuses.

1. TWO FURTHER FACULTY PORTRAITS

MOHAMMED DAJANI

In March 2014, Al-Quds University faculty member Mohammed Suleiman Dajani Daoudi (1946–) took twenty-seven of his Palestinian students from the campus to Poland to visit Auschwitz. Dajani had joined the Al-Quds faculty in east Jerusalem in 2001 and the following year established its American Studies Institute. Dajani was born in Jerusalem into a historic Arab family long embedded in the city's history; the honorific "Daoudi" was added to the family name in 1529 when Suleiman the Magnificent appointed a Dajani ancestor keeper of the Tomb of David on Mount Zion. Two Dajanis served as Jerusalem mayor between 1863 and 1918; Hassan Sidiqui Dajani, a lawyer, was assassinated in 1938 for heading the opposition to the Grand Mufti Haj Amin el-Husseini and advocating Arab-Jewish reconciliation. The Mufti later allied himself with Adolf Hitler.

As a student at the American University of Beirut after the Six-Day War, Mohammed Dajani was active in the PLO's Fatah but in 1975 he abandoned politics, "after witnessing a lot of corruption and misuse of funds in Fatah and losing hope in the Fatah cause" (Nurding). He studied at Eastern Michigan University, the University of South Carolina, and the University of Texas at Austin. He found his first teaching job in 1985 teaching political science in Jordan. But when the Palestinian National Authority was established a decade later he "joined the UN Development Program and was put in charge of setting up the PA ministries and the training centers for the new Palestinian civil ser-vants" (Nurding). Two years later, he joined the PA as a consultant and then became Director of Technical Assistance and Training. None of that history of commitment counted for anything when he transgressed by taking his students to visit Auschwitz.

As I detail below, his experiences with Israeli medicine changed his attitude toward both Jews and the Jewish state. Dajani had been involved in reconciliation efforts for nearly twenty years before the Auschwitz experience, so the trip reflected a long-term commitment. He had first seen Auschwitz himself in 2011, afterwards coauthoring a 2011 *New York Times* op-ed titled "Why Palestinians Should Learn about the Holocaust."

The trip to the most well-known death camp was part of "Hearts of Flesh—Not Stone," a collaborative educational program designed to teach each side about the historical suffering that shaped the narrative of the other. Dajani was working in a joint program on Reconciliation and Conflict Resolution with the Friedrich Schiller University in Jena, Germany, and Ben-Gurion University of the Negev. Al-Quds University was not an institutional participant. The Israeli students in the program visited the Dheisheh refugee camp just south of Bethlehem in the West Bank. Established as a temporary refuge in 1949, the camp increasingly acquired the accoutrements of permanence, though a por-tion of it had yet to be connected to a public sewage system. As *Haaretz* reported, "He says the choice of Dheisheh for the Israeli students was not meant to suggest there was an equivalence or even a direct link between the Holocaust and the Nakba. They were chosen as the sym-bolic events that have deeply affected the psyche on both sides of the conflict." The aim was to build mutual empathy and understanding through an appreciation of events central to the other side's narratives and self-understanding.

In a Jerusalem café in spring 2016, I spent most of a day with Dajani, during which he made it clear that he knew he had to discuss the trip with others in advance. That included the Al-Quds University president, Sari Nusseibeh. Accounts of that conversation differ. Dajani understood himself to have Nusseibeh's approval for the trip, though the president had also instructed him to tell the students that Al-Quds had nothing to do with it. But in the aftermath of the trip, when it became highly controversial, Nusseibeh denied having given his approval. Two members of the Al-Quds administration who discussed the events with me in August 2016 differed in their understandings as well; one supported Nusseibeh's account, the other confirmed Dajani's.

In any case, plans for the trip became public knowledge beforehand, and Dajani was pressed to cancel it. Warnings about the consequences came from multiple political and paramilitary groups both overtly and covertly active in East Jerusalem and the West Bank, including Fatah and Hamas. But Dajani was determined to honor his commitment. On his last day at Auschwitz, Dajani received an email from his secretary. As Dajani told *Moment* magazine editor Nadine Epstein, "Students marched to my office holding placards that said: 'Depart you normalizer,' and handed my secretary a letter warning me not to come back to the university." The students had trashed her office when they delivered the letter. A Palestinian journalist called him "the king of normalizers." On his return, hostility escalated. The Israeli newspaper *Haaretz* broke the story about the trip. The fact that the trip was part of a collaborative program did not help win approval among anti-Israel opponents of "normalization." Dajani, moreover, was already unpopular for opposing the effort to boycott Israeli universities.

None of this played well on the Palestinian street. Holocaust deniers asserted that Dajani was trying to brainwash his students by disseminating the fabrication that the Holocaust was real. He was denounced as a traitor and collaborator by students and others and warned not to enter Ramallah. The faculty union canceled his membership. Dajani had expected the university to expel the students who threatened his life. Instead, Al-Quds publicly distanced itself from the trip, claiming it was altogether a personal venture. Nonetheless, Dajani felt he should give the institution a chance to honor his academic freedom by defending his right to his pedagogical practices. He offered his resignation on May 18, 2014, anticipating it would be rejected. Instead, he immediately found himself out of a job as of June 1. Dajani summarized these events in a 2016 Washington Institute interview with Mical Polacco: "In March 2014, the Workers, Staff, and Faculty Syndicate at Al-Quds University fired me from their membership. Nine political student organizations on campus issued a public statement against me titled 'Normalization = Treason.' Students demonstrated against me on campus and delivered a letter to my secretary threatening to kill me if I returned to teach at the university" (Dajani "Why Palestinians").

According to Dajani, as he told me in our conversation, news accounts of the most dramatic subsequent event misrepresented its character. In January 2015, it was reported that his car was set on fire and destroyed while it was parked in front of his house. (For many, that recalled the occasion when Birzeit University President Hanna Nasir was attacked and injured and his car burned in November 1993 after he announced that the Islamic Bloc had won the contested student council election.)[12] Widely understood to be a threat and a warning that he must leave, Dajani now insists that it was far more serious. In the account he offered in 2016, highly experienced operatives—possibly working through a trained student group—poured a flammable glue into the spaces between the metal segments of the car. The glue was designed to burst into flame when the car was started and the engine began to warm. Luckily for Dajani, an unexpectedly warm day intervened, and the car burst into flame and burned up before he had occasion to drive it himself. Published photos of the car show that the fire was concentrated at the front around the engine. It was not a warning; it was an assassination attempt. His pedagogy had nearly proven fatal. He fled to West Jerusalem where he would be safe. Subsequently he took up residence in Washington DC, as the inaugural Weston Fellow at the Washington Institute, though he is working on plans to return to Jerusalem to start a doctoral program in reconciliation studies. He has not given up hope nor his principles, though he now understands the risks that Palestinian faculty can face when they voice unpopular political opinions.

A soft-spoken and dignified advocate at once of Palestinian rights and a negotiated peace, Dajani believes that contact and conversation between Israelis and Palestinians and the cultivation of mutual empathy are necessary preconditions for a resolution of the conflict. But achieving

---

12. Hanna Nasir, a physicist who was Birzeit's first president, was expelled to Lebanon by Israeli authorities in 1974. He moved to Jordan and remained president-in-exile until he was allowed to return to Birzeit and resume his post in 1993.

empathy requires breaking taboos; hence the Auschwitz trip. Dajani came to this view from a personal history that began with antagonism. As a young engineering student at the American University of Beirut in the 1960s, he was active in Fatah. He headed the group, and saw that kind of political activism as the only route to liberation, but was deported from Lebanon in 1975. Also exiled by Israel from his native Jerusalem and banned from Jordan because of his political activities, he pursued his education in the United States, earning a BA in Economics from Eastern Michigan University. He then completed two doctorates, one in Government from the University of South Carolina and one in Political Economy from the University of Texas at Austin.

He was only allowed to return to Israel in 1993 when his father was being treated for cancer. Like many Palestinians who have contact with Israeli medicine, he was surprised when it became clear that Jewish doctors saw his father not as an enemy but as a patient and a human being. The experience was repeated when his mother became ill. But most Palestinian students, lacking family members with serious illnesses, do not have these characteristically transformative contacts with Israeli medicine. Instead, they learn distrust and resentment when they spend hours waiting in lines at checkpoints on their way to campus. As a faculty member at Al-Quds, he sought to break the pattern with an educational experiment. However, neither his views nor his pedagogy were acceptable for Palestinian faculty; they are not protected by academic freedom. This time it was his fellow Palestinians who forced him into exile. Along with three others, including his brother Munther, he has since coedited *Teaching Empathy and Reconciliation in the Midst of Conflict* (2016). The book is published by Wasatia Press, a project of Wasatia, an organization promoting Islamic traditions of nonviolence and compromise that the Dajani brothers cofounded in 2007.

As he remarks to Sam Nurding, "I thought of establishing a political party, the Wasatia Party, but I came under attack by both Fatah and Hamas, who accused me of taking money from US intelligence services to 'Westernize Islam,' which of course was not true!" Dajani continues to work for peace, convinced that "Palestinians and Israelis should humanize the image of the other in his/her mind and build bridges of communication" (Nurding); he just cannot pursue this goal from

East Jerusalem or the West Bank. Nor can he do so from a Palestinian university.

ABDUL SATTAR QASSEM

In late January 2016, Professor Abdul Sattar Qassem (or Abdul al-Sattar Qassam, 1948–), a political scientist who has taught at An-Najah National University in Nablus for three decades, was arrested by the Palestinian Authority at his home on charges of inciting violence against the group's leaders. As Palestinian-Israeli journalist Khaled Abu Toameh reported in the *Jerusalem Post*, "Fatah accused Qassem of calling for the killing of Abbas and members of the PA security forces for their alleged collaboration with Israel. In an interview with the Hamas-affiliated Al-Quds TV station, Qassem called for the implementation of the PLO's 'Revolutionary law,' which imposes a death sentence on those found guilty of 'high treason ("Palestinian Forces").'" Of course, these would be actionable offenses in Western countries as well, but Qassem denies the charges, which, according to the Palestinian Centre for Human Rights, included "slandering prominent figures and inciting sectarian feuds." A number of groups, including Islamic Jihad, described the arrest as political, a claim that the Ma'an News Agency reports the PA denied, and called for his immediate release. That release took place a few days later.

Qassem is in every respect the opposite of Dajani. Opposed to reconciliation with Israel, he faced persecution and assaults on his life for quite different political beliefs. Unlike Dajani, moreover, he is not personally opposed to violence.

Qassem was born in the Tulkarem-area village of Deir al-Ghusoun in the northern West Bank. He earned a bachelor's degree in political science from American University of Cairo in 1972, during which time he sought to become involved with the Palestine liberation movement. As he remarked in a 2009 *Electronic Intifada* interview with Marcy Newman, "I wanted to be part of the revolution. I used to call it a revolution; I discovered later that it wasn't. I went to Beirut three times: in 1970, 1971, and 1972 to join a Palestinian faction. Each time I was disappointed and left without joining. I noticed that they were not true revolutionaries." He went on to earn a master's degree in economics and a doctorate in political science from the University of Missouri.

In 2004, Qassem was briefly a self-declared candidate for the Palestinian presidency, though he withdrew in a letter to the Central Elections Commission that accused both local media and the international community of unfairly favoring Mahmoud Abbas.

A regular columnist for *Al Jazeera's* Arabic-language website about Palestinian and Arab affairs, Qassem has a long history of incendiary views and a history as well of being arrested for them. According to IMRA, he posted a call to kidnap Israelis for prisoner exchanges to the official Hamas Internet site on August 20, 2004.[13] In April 2009 he was arrested by Palestinian security forces. In August 2011 he was again arrested by the PA security forces after his university filed libel charges against him. He had accused the university of corruption and had published a piece accusing the institution of failing to execute a court order blocking the expulsion of four students. A 2011 article by Khalid Amayreh on The Palestinian Information Center's website describes him as "one of the most courageous and outspoken intellectuals in occupied Palestine" and adds that "the PA justice system and leadership don't really see any difference between defamation and slander on the one hand and legitimate freedom of expression and speech on the other." According to Budour Youssef Hassan in *The Electronic Intifada*, which writes approvingly of him, "Qassem survived an assassination attempt by unknown gunmen shortly after being released from his latest stint in Israeli prison, where he spent a week in July 2014; he was shot in his car, while driving to give a television interview condemning Israel's massive military assault on Gaza at the time." Four bullets struck his legs and hand. Following his pattern of attacking both Israel and the PA, a year earlier he had given an interview to the Arabic-language newspaper

---

13. IMRA translates an An-Najah thesis by Yassir Mahmoud 'Ali Abu Bakr, directed by Qassem, about "the willingness of (Palestinian) Muslims to sacrifice their lives and detonate themselves and die for the sake of Allah to kill their enemies." He also "participated in shooting attacks, laid explosive charges and transmitted weapons and explosive belts to suicide bombers." He quotes Qassem as an authority.

Al-Sinnarah declaring Israel no longer "an unbeatable power" and urged Hezbollah to attack because it "has the ability to neutralize the Israeli air force."[14] Hassan adds that "A coalition of civil society organizations and some political factions are protesting Qassem's arrest, putting out a statement calling for his immediate release as part of the [Palestinian] 'commitment to preserve civil liberties and defend freedom of expression.'" Hassan's piece was occasioned by Qassem's arrest yet again by the Palestinian Authority in February 2016.

In the 2009 interview, in which he reported being shot at and wounded in 1995, accusing Yasser Arafat of trying to silence him, Qassem argued, "I cannot just stay silent while the PA rapes my land, my country and my people. They are collaborating with the Israelis. They are coordinating with them on security matters. They have been arresting Palestinians in defense of Israeli security" (Marcy Newman). As Raeed N. Tayeh reports, in 1999 Qassem and twenty others signed a petition laying out their grievances against the PA and implicating Arafat in its "corruption, abuse of power, misuse of resources, human rights violations, and a dysfunctional political process." The title of the article is "Jailed Professor Talks About Palestinian Authority's Intolerance of Criticism," a key issue in this essay. In total, Qassem spent eight months in prison on three separate charges of attacking Arafat. While academic freedom would protect Qassem from university sanctions for his statements (excepting any proven incitements to violence), it is notable that the Palestinian Authority has not historically been inclined to grant any special consideration to its most severe academic critics for ordinary criticism of its policies and leadership. That constitutes yet one more contribution to the chilling effect on free expression at Palestinian universities.

---

14. I am quoting from the WikiLeaks released Global Intelligence Files, in which the company Stratfor provides translations of Arabic publications.

2. THE ESTABLISHMENT OF PALESTINIAN UNIVERSITIES: ACADEMICS VS. ACTIVISM

Within a few years of its 1967 victory in the Six-Day War, Israel recognized both the need for a true Palestinian higher education system and the Palestinian right to have one. During the twenty years from 1948-1967 when Jordan occupied the West Bank and Egypt occupied Gaza, neither nation supported any such initiative. Thus there were no Palestinian universities throughout that period. Indeed, Jordan itself did not have a university until 1962. As Antony Sullivan emphasized in a 1991 essay,

> neither Jordan nor Egypt made any effort to encourage such interest, fearful as they were of Palestinian separatist sentiment in the territory which they had incorporated or begun to administer after 1948 . . . . These and other Arab countries feared that a distinctive Palestinian nationalism—especially in its terroristic incarnation—posed a challenge which might result in their social and political destabilization. (251)

Both Jordan and Egypt, in other words, recognized that Palestinian higher education would offer opportunities for wider destabilizing political consciousness-raising, political organizing, and lethal violence. It could impact Jordan and Egypt themselves.

A distinctive Palestinian identity began to cohere after 1967; as Nusseibeh writes, "Arabs were becoming self-consciously 'Palestinian'" (173). Along with population growth and difficulty traveling to study in other countries, that strengthened national identity helped motivate Palestinians to create their own universities. As a Palestinian identity began to cohere, Palestinians increasingly realized that foreign universities in Egypt, Jordan, Lebanon or elsewhere could not be expected to preserve, enhance, and promote Palestinian culture.[15] They would need their own universities. Palestinian universities "built aspirations, hopes, and ambitions . . . . Palestinian universities have encouraged young people to be Palestinians" (Alfoqahaa 26, 27). As the European Commission points out, "these institutions were part of a Palestinian collective effort to preserve their identity as well as to provide young Palestinians with the opportunity to pursue HE" [higher education] (3).

Over time, Palestinian higher education had another important impact on Palestinian culture because most colleges and universities are coeducational. As Palestinians have noted, that increased general (but not universal) acceptance of women in the workplace. Yet horrific honor killings of women continue to occur (Honour Based Violence; Palestinian Center). Since this topic comes up later in this paper, I will add that I believe it should be a matter of ethical principle that honor killings or other forms of exceptional violence against women not be discounted or minimized as instances of cultural relativism. Nor should criticism of them be dismissed as Islamophobia.

Although I will be reviewing the whole history of Palestinian higher education, it is important to keep in mind that its current phase and prevailing conditions date from initial steps in the implementation of the Oslo Accords, with the Palestinian Authority (PA) taking responsibility for higher education in 1994. As a result of the Oslo Accords and as a consequence of the Early Transfer of Authority Agreement between the Palestinian Liberation Organization (PLO) and Israel, the Palestinian Ministries of Education and Higher Education came into

---

15. Ibrahim Abu Lughod offers another motivation for establishing Palestinian universities: "Palestinian recognition that their 1948 defeat (and the defeat of the Arab states) by Israel was in part related to the superior education of their adversary" (81).

existence in August 1994 (European Commission). The PA became responsible for overall regulation, centralized financing, much fundraising, and security on the campuses. The Palestinian Ministry of Education and Higher Education, combined in 1996, has those responsibilities except for those assigned to the security services. Although Palestinian education is chronically underfunded, its annual budget has been periodically increased, growing, for example from USD 40 million in 2010 to USD 90 million the following year, though not all allocations have actually been disbursed.[16] Universities enjoy academic autonomy and self-management, overseeing admissions, recruitment, assessment, degree awarding, and facilities development. Since 1994, Palestinian higher education has been significantly expanded to meet increased demand, but that has made maintaining standards difficult. Enrollment doubled between 1994/95 and 2001 alone. In 2003, Hashweh and Berryman worried that the quality of higher education was declining (31-55).[17] On the other hand, the creation of a series of specialized MA programs over the last generation has made important contributions to Palestinian society possible.

Given Palestinian higher education's demonstrated ability to provide graduates qualified to fill many necessary medical, technical, administrative, commercial, and service positions in West Bank society, it is clear there is no lack of serious instructional work ongoing on their campuses. There have also been improvements in the curriculum. Writing in 2000, Ibrahim Abu Lughod wrote that "graduate education is in the early stage of development and cannot sustain serious research" (85), but progress has been made since then. The steady increase in

---

16. One component of underfunding is that almost no students repay their educational loans (European Commission 5).

17. Koni et al (2012) complain that most evaluations of Palestinian higher education rely exclusively on quantifiable evidence, ignoring qualitive forms of analysis. That certainly applies to the very detailed USAID study. The Koni et al study is based on questionnaires distributed to two West Bank universities. They report high student satisfaction, despite dissatisfaction with computing services and the availability of faculty.

faculty publications over the last decade, after years of relatively weak research output, also suggests a positive impact on instruction.[18]

Some Palestinians have politicized the initial motives for creating a higher education system in a way that may reflect retroactive wishful thinking. Writing retrospectively, the author of a biography of Birzeit University's 1974–1993 Acting President Gabi Baramki (1929–2012) on the Palestinian Journeys website says "The building of the first national university under the yoke of a colonialist occupation intent on uprooting the land's original inhabitants was simultaneously a challenge to the occupying power, a refined cultural response in the face of segregationist policies, and an act of resistance to occupation, aimed at restoring the rights of Palestinians in their homeland." Former Birzeit faculty member and dean of students Munir Faseh echoes Baramki's sentiment, writing that Birzeit "sprang from a spirit of rebelliousness against any attempt to crush people" (33).

Other Palestinians, writing as well from a distance from the actual events, were uncomfortable ascribing any admirable motives for Israel's support and so describe Israel's cooperation as an effort at normalizing the occupation, as if universities would quiet Palestinian political aspirations, as opposed to having the opposite effect. That the IDF lawyers involved, some of them educated in the US and witnesses to Vietnam-era campus turmoil, would have any such confidence, is unlikely. From the outset, the Israelis knew that higher education would increase Palestinians' political aspirations. Meanwhile, high unemployment among Palestinian university graduates, especially during the Intifadas, did not promote gratitude for existing political and economic conditions. The high unemployment crisis has continued, abetted by poor coordination between the jobs available and student choice of majors. As the European Commission reported about Palestinian higher education

---

18. In their study of An-Najah faculty publications, Sweileh et al point out that the most active publishing fields there are medicine, followed by "chemistry, environmental sciences, and engineering" (6). Fine arts, humanities, and law "ranked low in their contributions to research output," with those faculty often publishing in local and regional venues that are not peer reviewed. There is reason to suppose that, just as in the West, these are the most politicized disciplines.

in 2012, "the high percentage of students studying social sciences (75%) is a major contributor to unemployment among graduates" (10).

In any case, the proposed institutions were "registered as charitable (non-profit) societies with the department of social affairs at the Israeli military authority" (Baramki). That gave them legal status. As Sullivan emphasizes, "The fact is that Israel did permit Palestinians to establish universities" (1991, 251). So far as I can determine, Israel did not fund the institutions, but it provided Palestinians with their legal basis.[19] Palestinians were then able to raise the necessary funds from Arab sources, both from area states and from the Palestinian diaspora worldwide. By the mid-1980s there were five Palestinian universities in the West Bank: Al-Quds, An-Najah, Bethlehem, Birzeit, and Hebron.[20] Now there are eight, along with numerous colleges. Israel now recognizes their degrees.[21]

While universities were not the only Palestinian institutions active during the 1970s—others ranged from charities to trade unions to

---

19. Roberts et al write: "An Israel government memorandum sent to the Director-General of UNESCO on 19 June 1981, summarized in the UNESCO Director-General's 30 August 1983 report, Annex IV, pp. 9-10, stated that the Israeli military administration had 'contributed to the budgets of some of these institutions'. This may have been so in the past. But we have no further details, and we have not seen the claim repeated more recently" (40). Lynne R. Franks writes that "Israel does not finance higher education but does contribute to the three government community colleges because of their involvement in teacher training programs" (230). I spent some time in Israel seeking clarification on this issue but was not successful.

20. An-Najah, located in Nablus with a majority Muslim student body of about 23,000, is the largest Palestinian University. Its name is variously written as An-Najah, Al-Najah, An-Najah National University, or simply Najah. Bethlehem University, a Catholic coeducational institution that collaborates with Laval University of Canada, began operating in 1973 following a Papal visit to the area. It was established by the de la Salle Brothers (Brothers of the Christian Schools), three of whom administered the institution, under the auspices of the Vatican. An American priest served as president. The Shaykh Muhammad Al Ja'abri College of Sharia Studies was established as a small Sharia (Islamic law) college in 1971, becoming Hebron University in 1980.

21. Gerner and Schrodt suggest that, in a Palestinian state, these universities could become a major regional resource and industry.

human rights organizations—universities nonetheless were probably the most significant institutions originating in the period. Christa Bruhn argues that they are "a unique manifestation of the university in that Palestinian universities serve as national institutions in the absence of a Palestinian state"; they "enabled Palestinians to express their identity and represent their interests" (1126). Eventually, universities would give Palestinians the opportunity to "engage with each other to reflect on their shared experience of displacement, dispossession, and exile" (1127) and "reflect on what it meant to be Palestinian . . . . Thus Palestinian universities empowered Palestinians to develop a Palestinian national consciousness that planted the seeds of social and political change" (1128, 1130).

What no one could have anticipated was the intensified politicization of these institutions during the First Intifada (1987–1991). Keith Hammond, a British faculty member who is comprehensively hostile to Israel, writes that "Palestinian universities came into being as contemporary degree conferring institutions in the 1970s but they did not function as 'Palestinian' universities until the first intifada in 1986" (265). As Bruhn writes, "Although the young boy in the street throwing stones at the Israeli army became the face of the Intifada, it was the university that translated those stones into an articulate appeal to the international community for an end to Israeli occupation" (1132). The First Intifada was the period when student-organized demonstrations spread off-campus and shouted slogans, burning tires, hurled rocks, and Molotov cocktails accompanied the building of barricades across city streets, practices now deeply ingrained and continuing to the present day (Figs. 5, 6). The IDF resorted to rubber bullets and live ammunition to restore public order and discourage similar future actions. A number of students were among those who lost their lives during these mass public actions in Palestinian cities, while others were killed on campus. Birzeit maintained and publicized lists of students killed, but did not differentiate in its lists between those killed on campus versus off campus. Student status is relevant in both cases, especially given that deaths occurred in public demonstrations that were student organized. Yet a death in a city center is not inherently an assault on higher education, despite sometimes being characterized that way. Nonetheless,

all those searing deaths proved unforgettable tragedies. They helped
define a generation's understanding of injustice and its basis for political
opposition.

As someone who was active in Vietnam protests for a decade and
worked in a confidential national program to help people escape the
draft, I still feel the shock of the Kent State shootings. But exceptional
deaths of one's peers may not threaten daily life and political expression
long-term in the same destructive way as the sense that your fellow
students and faculty surveil your views in order to impose political
conformity. Palestinian enforcement of political conformity defines the
limits of academic freedom at Palestinian universities.

Campuses were repeatedly closed down, sometimes for months, most
often by the IDF but sometimes by the universities themselves to quell
internal disputes. The longest closure by far was the one Israel imposed
from January 10, 1988, to the fall of 1991, with Birzeit remaining closed
until April 29, 1992. That the long closure especially abnegated academic freedom for its duration is without question. Birzeit University's
The Criminalization of Education, Academic Freedom . . . (1989) exhaus-
tively details why that was true, beginning with the denial of access
to academic libraries and on-campus research labs, the cancellation of
on-campus classes, and the loss of opportunities for academic exchange.
"Academic freedom, after all," the ninety-page report begins in an
overly broad definition, "is the right to study and teach without outside
interference" (22). But it is not unfair to say that IDF policies effectively
treated "education itself as a criminal activity" (3); it was not literally
so defined, and it did not permanently define working conditions at
Palestinian universities, but education was effectively suppressed. Yet it
is not true that "closures and other forms of punishment directed at the
University were undertaken precisely because the University was fulfill-
ing its function as a genuine university, a forum for the free exchange
of ideas" (4). Palestinian universities unfortunately never have been and
still are not simply sites of intellectual exchange. Birzeit's claim is propaganda. In retrospect, all Palestinian higher education stakeholders have
been proud to claim universities as the core of the uprising, especially in
its opening months, but nowhere in *The Criminalization of Education,
Academic Freedom* is that central fact even mentioned, let alone the fact,

as documented thoroughly elsewhere in this paper, that campus groups fomented and organized terrorism. Palestinian universities are treated exclusively as politically innocent purveyors of knowledge. The IDF felt it had to close universities both to block specific terrorist activities and to prevent an armed uprising. It also hoped the loss of education would build popular opposition to the Intifada. There are other inaccuracies. While the IDF did declare the alternative classrooms held in homes and mosques illegal, for the most part it tolerated them. The main principle, however, is that "Palestinian society has the right to administer, regulate, and build its own educational institutions under its own authority" (79), a right finally obtained in 1994. The long closure of 1988-1992 has happily not been repeated in nearly thirty years.

Despite the years that have passed, the anti-Zionist BDS movement continues to cite the closures of the 1980s as reason to sanction Israel in the present day. As recently as June 2020, a BDS coalition in the Society for the Study of Social Problems (SSSP) submitted a resolution for the academic group's annual meeting (scheduled as a virtual event in response to the coronavirus pandemic) proposing a boycott of Israeli universities. Among the purportedly evidentiary "whereas" clauses in the resolution is "Whereas, Israeli military authorities have closed Palestinian universities and destroyed cultural and academic institutions." The clause footnotes a Birzeit University list of closures initiated between 1973 and 1988, the most serious taking place during the First Intifada. This is one of several clauses suggesting that Israeli universities should be punished for government actions in which the universities played no role. The resolution, moreover, says nothing about the role Palestinian universities played in the uprising.

Writing in 1987, Penny Johnson, assistant to Birzeit's public relations director and later a cofounder of and researcher in its Institute of Women's Studies, admits somewhat euphemistically that "the universities remain as the primary locus for expressions of Palestinian nationalism" (D-135). Albert Aghazarian, former director of its Public Relations Office, describes Birzeit as "a sort of polarizing beacon in Israel." Students declared Birzeit a "liberated zone" at the time (Johnson G-102). "Universities, particularly Birzeit University, became the focus of nationalist events; mass rallies there and in other institutions became

a potent instrument of politicization and mobilization during this
period" (Taraki 61). At least some faculty played a role in the network
of popular committees that sustained the uprising. Palestinians found
their fundamental understanding of the purpose of higher education
changing. Sari Nusseibeh reports that he had worked to avoid political
advocacy in the classroom: "I did my best to keep education and politics
separate" (160). But now he found politics and pedagogy converging:
"Education is a tool to prevent people from passively stewing in their
own resentment, and either giving up by submitting or lashing out by
tossing bombs" (181).

Palestinian student activism was shaped and often controlled by the
elected student councils, which had then and continue to wield substantially more influence and power than student governments in Europe
and the US. Indeed, "every institution today has a dean of students,
whose role is quite political; he works closely with the student council"
(Lughod 91). As Penny Johnson reports from Birzeit, in those institutions roiled by competition for control of the student government,
"political polarization exists at all levels of the university and the institutional structure is a reflection of that reality" (Johnson F-147). As she
fairly points out, however, "under occupation, normal academic processes become infused with political content" (A-128). Antony Sullivan
elaborates on this principle in his book on the subject:

> Palestinians understandably look to their institutions of higher
> learning to produce the leadership that will resist further Israeli
> settlement in the occupied Territories, discourage continued Israeli
> seizure of Palestinian land and water resources, and challenge the
> arrest and imprisonment of Palestinian nationalists by the Israeli
> occupation authorities. Palestinian politics, then, is ineluctably
> associated with Palestinian education. (22)

Yet such expectations, as we have begun to see, tend to eliminate
tolerance for alternative viewpoints, create coercive and threatening
environments as a consequence, and impose severe limits on academic
freedom. Moreover, Sullivan's list of honorable political activities does
not exhaust the reality. When Birzeit faculty member Eileen Kuttab
assures us that the institution's "core aims include the promotion
of political tolerance and respect for different views" (164), she is

simply offering specious verbiage for a Western audience. When she adds that what are notoriously coercive and violent student council elections "internalize democratic processes into [university] governance structures" she crosses the line into active deception. When Jimmy Carter echoes that claim, saying that "student council elections have provided generations of Palestinian leaders with practical experience in democracy," the enabling mechanism is more likely self-deception (ix). Part of what is actually normalized in these election campaigns is the expectation that physical intimidation and assault are integral to political debate and democratic process. We expect democratic process to instill the opposite conviction.

From the late 1970s until the present, the results of these violently contested student council elections sometimes underwent continual reversal, though the Islamic Bloc and Hamas also had periods of repeated success. The 1979 election at An-Najah saw the Islamic Bloc win ten of eleven seats. The following year the National Unity Bloc representing PLO factions won six, with the Islamic Bloc holding five. In 1981 the Islamic Bloc swept the field. In 1986, the Student Youth Movement, supporting Fatah, received 1,480 votes, compared to the Islamic Bloc's 1,160 (Abu-Amr 17). These elections are frequently cited as indicators of broader Palestinian opinion. Whether or not that is true, the political and paramilitary groups certainly see the wide value—in terms of opportunities for publicity, recruitment, and organizing—of winning student council elections, which is one reason they are willing to invest time and resources into the contests.

Those promoting the role of higher education in Palestinian society are often more inclined to treat Palestinian universities as seamlessly unified ideologically and politically. Munir Faseh writes that at Birzeit there were "no boundaries between the administration, teachers, and students" (31), but then his claim is included in a large format edited book produced by Birzeit's Public Relations Office, *Birzeit University: The Story of a National Institution*. The book problematically combines an account of the institution's history and development with expressions of political solidarity and PR efforts to promote the university. The mix of motives does not make for uniform reliability.[22]

However, we often find that, as with universities elsewhere, different stakeholders have competing interests and are sometimes at odds with one another. The consequences of real conflicts between Palestinian stakeholders are frequently serious. For example, faculty/student conflicts with the administration and labor-management disputes familiar in the West are intensified. Faced with financial pressures, Palestinian universities in the 1980s increased tuition. At Birzeit, students argued "either that there is no financial crisis or that the measures taken to solve it are designed to reinstitute the university as an institution serving only the elite in Palestinian society and to weaken its nationalist character" (Johnson A-133). Faculty protested that "the board to date had never presented the university staff with a full picture of the financial crisis or solicited their participation in fund-raising and financial planning" (Johnson B-121). Such conflicts might seem familiar from the US, but they were more serious when universities said they couldn't meet payroll. A 1986 faculty/employee strike lasted forty-five days. In the same period there were strikes over tuition increases at both Birzeit and Hebron. An-Najah University was closed down for two months in the 1987-1988 academic year in response to a dispute between fundamentalist and nationalist students. It reopened for two weeks but then closed again because of conflict over a tuition increase. These were all internal decisions. "Closure has become the immediate response to internal problems at An-Najah" (Johnson F-103-4).

It would be foolish to imagine that Palestinian universities could exist in an academicized bubble floating free of engagement with the occupation. Perhaps that was what the Israeli military authorities imagined when they established a list of books to be banned from Palestinian campuses that grew to approximately 350 titles by the mid-1980s according to Antony Sullivan (1991, 265) and to a thousand titles according to Raja Shehadeh (185). Whatever the size of the list, it clearly

---

22. Long-term Birzeit faculty member Roger Heacock writes that "The Public Relations Office was, in the pre-Oslo period, the nodal point of concerted action to protect the life of the community and the very existence of the institution . . . . It was through that office in large part that solidarity passed" (74).

abridged academic freedom, though the libraries regularly ignored it and obtained books without Israeli approval. As Adam Roberts and his coauthors point out,

> Like so much censorship, it contains an element of the absurd. Some of the titles that West Bank institutions are not permitted to acquire are available in the library of Hebrew University of Jerusalem, where members of West Bank universities [at the time could] consult them. Some of the titles that cannot be sold in Ramallah can be bought quite openly in Jerusalem. Some of the titles that are banned in Arabic are available in English. (65)

In fact, as Antony Sullivan points out, the Birzeit "library's social science and Middle East sections feature an impressive range of works by orientalists, Jewish and Israeli scholars, and Western political scientists and historians . . . in addition to a range of works by Arab scholars" (36). He provides a list of representative titles in the collection, then does the same for An-Najah's library (*Under Occupation* 50).

The authority to ban books was included in Military Order 854, adapted from Jordanian Law No. 16 and issued by the IDF on July 6, 1980. It was signed by Brigadier General Binyamin Ben-Elizer, the Israeli commander of the Judea and Samaria region. As Samir Anabtawi writes in what is the most thoughtful review of Palestinian higher education in the 80s,

> It requires universities to submit to censorship in curricular offerings and the acquisition of books, and demands that faculty members sign a statement that they would not either directly or indirectly support the PLO. Those refusing to do so are threatened with the loss of their work permits and their physical expulsion from the West Bank. (30)

Gabi Baramki in 2010 and Penny Johnson in her 2018 essay describe several non-violent forms of non-cooperation that Palestinian universities adopted as resistance tactics. One of the more interesting of these was the Birzeit decision to remove the clause (no. 18) disavowing membership in the PLO from a form nonresident faculty were required to sign. Administrators recopied the document without the clause and the Israeli authorities did not initially notice its absence. After further dispute, Israel stopped enforcing the clause and provided a revised form omitting it. It is worth noting, however, that the actual force driving non-cooperation was not the university administration: "noncompliance stemmed from the objections of students, who unequivocally refused to study under any lecturer that signed the request in its current form" (Zelkovitz 109). Once again, students exercised agency and influence.

Among those arguing that Order 854 granted powers that violated academic freedom were five Hebrew University professors who issued a detailed report on it in 1981 (Gavison et al), though most of Order 854's provisions were never implemented (Roberts 61). "As a rule the Israeli authorities have not intervened directly in detailed academic matters such as development of the curriculum, examining and so on" (Roberts 68). Nor did the Israelis try to control research agendas. But some Palestinians nevertheless saw Order 854 "as a 'sword of Damocles' hanging over the universities" (62). Such fears entailed an element of hyperbole, as with the claim that "Israeli Authorities have the power simply to confiscate the universities' libraries whenever they choose to do so" or the relief that Israelis "have not yet officially closed any of them [universities] permanently" (Sullivan *Under Occupation* 15, 2). Order 854 did, however, succeed in generating a good deal of negative publicity for Israel, some of it encouraged, Roberts and his coauthors speculate, because "the universities might have an interest in appearing to be persecuted" (71). Order 854 was misguided and is an important part of the historical record, but it has been moot for over twenty-five years. This includes its book banning component, since the Oslo Accords came into effect in 1994 and responsibility for Palestinian higher education was transferred to the Palestinian Authority.

The creation and growth of their universities may be the single greatest Palestinian achievement, but university development has been hampered by cultural values that have been difficult to overcome. Sullivan notes that in Palestinian higher education "rational processes for decision-making are in short supply" (*Under Occupation* 47). As Anabtawi, a Palestinian with wide international educational experience describes it, these institutions have been burdened with "an administrative machinery which seeks obeisance to a stifling uniformity" (16). As he details, there is a "system of university governance which gave little executive latitude to those officials who were supposed to be in charge"

(40) and instead "calls for the creation of innumerable and multi-layered controlling devices for the ratification of every conceivable act" (44). There are "hosts of rules that seek to define and regulate everyone's prerogative and conduct during every contingency and at every turn" (45).

This "pattern is conditioned by authoritarian decision-making structures that have their inception in the family and which are then magnified in the institutional mechanisms of religion and state" (33). Governing boards are given excessive authority and, as they include many parochial local area members, they find it easy to meddle. "No cross-regional board was established in any of the universities" (Zelkovitz 118). Some board members have lifetime appointments. At Birzeit, "many of the trustees were related by kinship or various other family ties" (Zelkovitz 118). Meanwhile, individual universities compete with one another for regional and international donors and sometimes disparage one another in the process. Since all the donors were Muslim, An-Najah found it useful to remind them that Birzeit's founders were Christian (Anabtawi 40).

As result, there exists no coordinated system of West Bank higher education that could pool resources and limit duplication of programs. The funds available are not expended in the most advantageous way. The Palestinian Authority has not yet solved this problem. Writing in the AAUP's magazine *Academe* in 2013, Mary Gray, in her third report on Palestinian higher education, finds some things unchanged: "Palestinian governmental and educational institutions must improve cooperation among themselves and convince local businesses to invest in education to serve the students, to continue to train and retain faculty members, and to provide the needed infrastructure."

Anabtawi is unstinting in his condemnation of the occupation and of the many ways it exacerbates some of the trends just enumerated, but Palestinian higher education's fundamental "difficulties do not lie in money, but in what they themselves have fashioned and wrought . . . . Nor does it lie in the harsh vicissitudes of occupation, as many so conveniently continue to allege" (82). The problem persists. Amy Kaplan quotes a Palestinian literature professor from a 2010 interview: "We don't like to blame ourselves, but we can't blame everything on occupation. We haven't made it a priority to build a critical research center at any of our universities." Both Palestinians themselves and their presumed allies in the BDS movement still resort to "attempts at exoneration for manifest shortcomings by pointing to the occupation as a rationale for educational deficiencies that do not in reality have their basis in foreign rule." They then "bolster each other's attitudes by gathering to lament and to commiserate" (52).

3. THE PALESTINIAN STUDENT MOVEMENT

From Paris in '68 to Hong Kong in 2019 we have seen campuses repeatedly in turmoil, as a unified student body clashed with police representing the authorities. But the level of student violence against other students and occasional assaults on faculty combine with lethal attacks on Israelis over decades to create a difference from these more well-known cases that is one of kind, not just degree.

Within half a decade of the founding of Palestinian universities, new students were subjected to increasingly intensive recruitment efforts by competing political factions. That practice continues today. At least since the Second (or Al-Aqsa) Intifada (2000–2005), entering students have received competing glossy brochures and indoctrination kits from each faction extolling its virtues, sometimes including the names and representative photographs of the shaheeds (martyrs) the faction or institution can claim as its own (IMRA).[23] "'Successful' terrorists become an icon—a 'saint'" (Community Security Trust 7) (Figs. 3, 12). Students killed in demonstrations, as well as suicide bombers, are included in those lists. Whether it was inevitable that suicide bombers be celebrated, as they are, I cannot say, but it is a political tradition with disastrous consequences. These celebrations "glorify and normalize extreme violence, as well as dehumanizing the victims which in turn potentially makes it easier for others to follow suit"; they create "an alternate reality in which terrorism offers purpose, fame and salvation" (Community Security Trust 10, 5). Of course, as one would

---

23. IMRA lists the contents of several propaganda and recruitment kits distributed at An-Najah in 2004.

expect, over the last generation active Palestinian student use of Islamic websites, documented in a study by An-Najah University journalism professor Farid Abudheir, has supplemented face-to-face interaction as a source of information. Political recruitment through social media is also prevalent, as it is globally. Livestreaming terrorist acts, pioneered by ISIS, has begun to infiltrate Hamas instigated terrorism.

The roots of Palestinian student political activism can be traced to the establishment of the General Union of Palestinian Students (GUPS) in 1959, which drew together Palestinian student associations "proliferating throughout Egypt, the Arab states, and Europe" (Zelkovitz 18).[24] Indeed, the student groups were the vanguards of the Palestinian national awakening, with GUPS organizing abroad to strengthen Palestinian national identity and later inspiring the student movement in the occupied territories. After the 1967 war, "GUPS leaders infiltrated the West Bank in order to establish underground military cells for the ongoing struggle against Israel" (94). A decade later "student cells began to form within institutions of higher education" (135).

The first student cells took form in the 1970s and were frequently communist-dominated. They were followed in the 1980s by the student branch of Fatah, "Shabiba," which was initially led mainly by former prisoners from Israeli jails now enrolled in higher education. (Fig. 7). They brought with them organizing capacities and political convictions. "Not only had the Israeli prison granted them the legitimacy of national heroes, but it had equipped them with practical leadership skills" (Zelkovitz 137). Shabiba "quickly emerged as the most potent force in the occupied territories" (Nusseibeh 150). Meanwhile, Fatah had decided to use university campuses as a training ground for its next generation of leaders. Unlike university boards of trustees, the student cells were not hampered by long traditions of clan politics and were thus better equipped for multi-campus coordination. They also gained respect by repairing and maintaining religious sites like cemeteries and mosques. Shabiba's ex-prisoners were also assigned "to recruit potential operatives from among the movement's members for underground

---

24. See Ido Zelkovitz's *Students and Resistance in Palestine: Books, guns and politics* for a detailed account of the international Palestinian student movement.

paramilitary actions" (Zelkovitz 139), a role Hamas currently assigns to its student cells.

The other most significant campus student movement in the 1980s was Islamist in inspiration and ideology, but it competed as well with the Popular Front for the Liberation of Palestine (PFLP), which inherited the radical left campus position from the Communist Party. The PFLP attracted a number of faculty members, which helped it organize students on some campuses. Conflicts between the three groups often turned violent. At the more conservative An-Najah campus, for example, hostility to the PFLP was well organized and led by the Islamic Bloc. The Islamic Bloc students embraced convictions that some faculty found unsettling. As Nusseibeh writes,

> In 1984 I noticed a change among some of my students. All the humiliations of their brief lives, tossed into a religious cauldron, had turned village boys, and sometimes girls, into implacable fanatics, hostile to the sort of liberty I was trying to teach them to love . . . ideological inebriation locked them into a narrow, unbending frame of mind. (220).

The consequences included not only fighting between political opponents but also battles within factions that were splintering:

> To a greater degree than other Palestinian universities, an-Najah has experienced factional fighting among student blocs.[25] During the early and mid 1980s such confrontations reflected divisions within the PLO subsequent to the Israeli invasion of Lebanon. The student body became so fragmented that there were "no longer merely leftist vs. rightist quarrels but battles between Fatah and Fatah, between those two and the Islamic movement, and between those three and the Democratic Front for the Liberation of Palestine, and the Communist Party. Even the three 'leftist' groups fought at times." At one point students from the Islamic Bloc clashed with students

---

25. In the years since Sullivan was writing, Islamic University, Al-Azhar, and Birzeit have matched An-Najah's record of factional violence. Sullivan's two internal quotations are both from pieces by Baher Ashab published in *Al Fajr*: "Student Factionalism Takes some Glimmer out of Campus Life" (March 28, 1986) and "Students, Administrators Lock Horns at Local Universities" (March 21, 1986).

from left-wing factions using daggers and chains. (Sullivan *Under Occupation* 52)

The clashes between student groups were supplemented by clashes with Israeli forces. Shabiba followed a well-planned strategy: a provoked "confrontation with soldiers at the university would erupt, followed by the school's closure, followed by a planned spreading out of students throughout villages and towns to mobilize for a more general strike" (Nusseibeh 200). Both internal Palestinian political disputes and the Intifadas included tactics and rhetoric that led students to cross the line repeatedly into violence. Both in the West Bank and Gaza, "The campuses served as gathering places and points of departure for mass riots, and as centers of tactical instruction for upcoming clashes" (Zelkovitz 153). As riots spread from campuses to the public sphere, the level of violence escalated. "In 1986, one of the assassins of Nablus mayor Zaafar al-Masri proved to be an an-Najah student" (Sullivan *Under Occupation* 52). Meanwhile, "the West Bank clashes stoked Israeli fears of an imminent, full-scale civil revolt" (Zelkovitz 153).

The line between academics and activism is inherently unstable, but unbridled faculty/student advocacy makes it worse. The line differentiating between violence and non-violence is the one campuses themselves must preserve and enforce. Palestinian universities failed (and continue to fail) to do so. No wonder the military authorities were often ambivalent about Palestinian higher education, oscillating between permissiveness and restraint. Their worries about politics getting out of control led the Israelis to try to micro-manage Palestinian universities, a project that largely failed.

Lynne Franks, of Queens College, who conducted a study of Israeli and Palestinian education on behalf of the American Association of Collegiate Registrars and Administrators in the mid-1980s, registered her frustration with the system at the time: "essentially anything and everything of any consequence with regard to the normal functioning of an academic institution require approval from the authorities" (229). As her own reporting demonstrates, however, that overstates the case. Thus she points that any new academic programs "must be approved by the military authorities," but then acknowledges that "once approved, there is little direct intervention in the setting of course curricula" (181).

As pointed out above, Israelis abandoned such requirements when the Oslo Accords went into effect in 1994 and overall responsibility was shifted to the new Palestinian Authority.

Immediately after the PA began to operate, however, it adopted some of the same practices many both locally and internationally had found objectionable on the part of the Israelis, including administrative detention. In 2001, Amnesty International acknowledged that the PA had held hundreds in administrative detention without trial, beginning in 1995, for as long as five to seven years. Amira Hass updated the fact in *Haaretz* in 2012. In 2017 the UN's Commissioner for Human Rights admitted it as well, though as briefly as possible. Human Rights Watch in 2018 reported that "the Palestinian Authority, which exercises limited autonomy in the West Bank, and Hamas authorities, who have de facto control inside the Gaza Strip, have cracked down on critical journalists, social media commentators, demonstrators, and university activists," employing administrative detention in the process. Reports of PA administrative detention of West Bank students in 2018 alone range from several score to as many as 400. Accurate statistics in this as in so many other areas are impossible to obtain, but the overall phenomenon is not in doubt. Once again, academic freedom was compromised.

4. BIRZEIT UNIVERSITY NEAR RAMALLAH

The oldest Palestinian university, established near Ramallah and now enrolling nearly 15,000 students, Birzeit evolved from a 1924 girls' elementary school owned by the Christian Arab Nasir family to become a two-year college with separate girls' and boys' schools in 1942. It became a university in 1975. The Nasir family transferred Birzeit from a private to a public institution supervised by a nonprofit nongovernmental foundation. A Board of Trustees took over in 1973. As Geoffrey Aronson writes,

> The change in status from a two-year junior college, first to a four-year institution and then to a full-fledged university, was accompanied by a change in the composition of the student body, from predominantly upper-class West Bank Christian Arabs, to students from all classes and denominations who were increasingly animated by the issues of occupation and independence. (187)

In September 2014, the Israeli journalist Amira Hass reported in *Haaretz* that she had been asked to leave a conference on "Alternatives to Neo-Liberal Development in the Occupied Palestinian Territories—Critical Perspectives" being held at Birzeit. The conference had been organized by the Rosa Luxemburg Foundation in Germany and The Center for Development Studies (CDS) at Birzeit. The two lecturers who asked Hass to leave explained that, for the past two decades, there had been a regulation at Birzeit stipulating that Jewish Israelis are not to be allowed on the university grounds. Hass had signed into the conference as a *Haaretz* reporter, one consistently sympathetic to the Palestinian cause and critical of the Israeli government. As she reported in *Haaretz*,

One of the lecturers explained that it is important for students to have a safe space where (Jewish) Israelis are not entitled to enter; that while the law is problematic, this was not the time or place to discuss amending it; and that, just as she could ask to treat me differently as an exception to the rule, another lecturer might ask for the same preferential treatment for Yossi Beilin, Israel's former justice minister who is known as one of the architects of both the Oslo Accords and Geneva Initiative and the initiator of the Taglit Zionist project. She also told me that Professor Ilan Pappé, author of the book *The Ethnic Cleansing of Palestine*, among others, had been invited to deliver a lecture at Birzeit, but owing to the law, gave the talk off campus. The other lecturer told me that if I didn't write "*Haaretz*" in the registration form, I would have been able to stay. Still another faculty member who I have known for 40 years walked past and said: "This is for your own protection [from the students]." Suffice it to say that Pappé's decision to cooperate with a discriminatory ban in violation of academic freedom was not an admirable one. The director of the Luxemburg Foundation later informed Hass that had she known of the prohibition against Jewish attendance, she would not have held the event on campus, but moving it off campus would also have been problematic. It is notable that one of the lecturers was arguing that an exception for a left-wing journalist like Hass could well lead to a similar request for an Israeli whose politics were unacceptable. One might well assume that this Palestinian teacher was either confused or poorly informed about the nature of academic freedom. However, as Amira Hass reported in *Haaretz*, the university itself issued a statement assuring everyone that "the administration has nothing against the presence of the journalist Hass. The university as a national institution differentiates between friends and enemies of the Palestinian people…and works with every person or institution that is against the occupation" (Hass "When"). That this statement was issued proudly is surely worth note.

Three days later the university strengthened its stance, declaring that it welcomed "supporters of the Palestinian struggle and opponents of the Israeli occupation of Palestine, regardless of nationality, religion, ethnicity, or creed." Cynically combining the standard language opposing discrimination with a political litmus test makes a compelling statement about the failure to honor academic freedom in Palestinian universities.

The problems with Birzeit's politicized caricature of academic freedom extend well beyond its willingness to discriminate against Zionists. Matthew Kalman comments in *Haaretz* in 2014 on the paradoxical character of life at Birzeit:

> I've reported from Birzeit dozens of times for *The Chronicle of Higher Education* and other media. I've reported the random arrests and administrative detention of their students and lecturers, often in the middle of the night, by the IDF. I've reported how many of those students and lecturers have been held for months, even years, without a fair trial, sometimes without even being told the crimes of which they are suspected.
>
> In 2009, for example, there were 83 Birzeit students incarcerated in Israeli jails, of whom 39 were convicted of various terror-related charges, 32 were awaiting trial, nine were in "administrative detention" and three were undergoing interrogation following their arrest. Birzeit accounts for more than half of all the 1,000 Palestinian students arrested by Israel since the start of the Second Intifada in 2000, including at least three of its student council heads who were arrested and held for months on end.
>
> Clearly, some of these students were also engaged in dangerous terrorist activity, but the majority appears to have been innocent of any real crime.
>
> Nor is Birzeit alone in feeling the crushing weight of Israel's occupation interfering daily with its studies and students. Just about every Palestinian university in the West Bank has stories of nighttime IDF raids, campus teargas attacks, and random arrests and intimidation.
>
> So I am well aware of the pressures that distinguish university life at Birzeit from Berkeley or Brooklyn College.
>
> But much of the trouble there has little to do with Israel or the occupation. I have also reported the political intimidation and violence doled out by some Birzeit students to their political opponents. I met the Islamist student who led the stone-throwing rioters who

injured the visiting French Prime Minister Lionel Jospin and chased him off campus in February 2000. The British Consul-General Sir Vincent Feane had to beat a similar retreat in 2013.

In 2007, university classes were suspended and students evacuated from the campus after Ahmad Jarrar, a student supporter of the ruling Fatah party, was assaulted in his dormitory room, apparently by four men from the Marxist PFLP. Jarrar was treated at a hospital for severe injuries suffered as he was apparently being tortured. The assailants used charcoal to burn Jarrar's face and hammered nails into his feet. Fatah gunmen arrived soon after, threatening to kill PFLP supporters.

More recently, Birzeit has tried to ameliorate its hostile student confrontations by negotiating with the powerful student groups. Ahead of the April 2019 student union elections, the university successfully sought agreement from the political bloc leaders to demilitarize their campaigns. But a few months later, when the same blocs were commemorating the sequential anniversaries of the PFLP, Hamas, and Fatah (December 11, December 14, and January 1), they refused to sign a charter banning "all displays of militarism, including the wearing of face masks and uniforms and the carrying of signs bearing slogans related to Palestinian resistance" (Z. Harel). The slogans endorsed armed struggle against Israel. The students insisted all this was merely "symbolic" and started to stage the marches anyway. "They noted that dozens of Birzeit students became prisoners and martyrs who left their mark on the history of Palestinian resistance, and that the university should continue to provide a political platform in praise of the Palestinian struggle" (Harel). "Hamas student bloc coordinator Abd Al-Rahman Alawi said: 'Birzeit University, whose alumni include the martyred 'engineer' Yahyah Ayyash, the imprisoned Marwan Al-Barghouti, and dozens of martyrs and prisoners who left their clear fingerprint on the history of the Palestinian resistance, must be a source of intifadas, and must serve as a political platform, as it does now" (Harel). Needless to say, intifadas are not merely "symbolic"; nor are calls for violence against Israelis. Celebrations of school martyrs are a form of incitement to violence (Figs. 8, 9, 12).

Faced with militarized demonstrations on December 1st and 16th, the university evacuated the campus on both occasions in 2019. "Following the dispersion of the two demonstrations, the student union boycotted classes, padlocked the gates of the university, and launched an open-ended sit-in on campus" (Harel). The employee union noted that models of weapons or missiles were among the displays that offended not only the Israeli authorities but also the university's donors. A student strike was initiated and lasted a month before a temporary truce was achieved.

In 2015, hundreds of Al-Quds university students attended the unveiling of a Christmas tree festooned with the pictures of dozens of terrorists (Shimon Cohen). Greek Orthodox Archbishop Atallah Hanna and the Mufti of Bethlehem Sheikh Abdul-Majid Ata Amarna removed the cover to the tree in a ceremony (Fig. 12). In 2016 another memorial to terrorists was erected at Al-Quds. "Written on the memorial stone was the sentence 'Beware of natural death; do not die, but amidst the hail of bullets'" (*Arutz Sheva* Staff). A senior Palestinian faculty member from Al Quds University bluntly described the conditions that Birzeit, Al-Quds, and other institutions confront in an August 2016 interview with me: "There is no academic freedom. Faculty members are afraid to speak their minds because they will be branded as traitors. Fatah, Hamas, and Islamic Jihad all have students available to harass and intimidate faculty who are so named. And sometimes their lives are put in danger." This generalization does not, of course, apply to all subject matter; it refers primarily to political speech, but what counts as political and which positions mark one politically encompass wider territory than in the West. As Bassem Eid, a Jerusalem-based Palestinian political rights activist, remarked to me in a 2016 conversation, what mosque you belong to identifies your political allegiances and shapes how your statements will be received. Indeed mosques commonly include a study circle that doubles as a political cell (Lybarger 97). This intersection of religion and politics presents life-threatening hazards in Palestinian society and throughout the Arab world. It is a major impediment to realizing a two-state solution.

Whatever Birzeit administrators actually know about academic freedom as it is understood in Europe, Israel, and North America is impossible to say, though it is likely that many do understand the way academic freedom is supposed to safeguard free expression of opinion. Yet it is nonetheless clear that they have historically not been willing to risk promoting, let alone enforcing, politically controversial standards that would provide an appropriate learning environment for students or the necessary minimum safeguards for faculty members. It is likely administrators fear the personal consequences of enforcing those standards. Can one blame them for a lack of physical and political courage in the face of factional violence, especially from a vantage point of physical safety in Europe and North America?

Most American academics generally neither understand nor care about the dual stresses that Palestinian students in both East Jerusalem and the West Bank experience. Both the IDF and Palestinian groups compromise academic freedom in various ways, but with far from equal severity. Yet the BDS movement criticizes only Israeli actions, ignoring the far more serious and dangerous assaults on a secure learning environment carried out by Palestinian factions and students themselves. Ignoring or misrepresenting the severity of the threats at stake means that US debates about academic freedom for Palestinian students and faculty are conducted in fundamental and corrupting ignorance.

5. STUDENT POLITICAL FACTIONS RECENTLY AT WAR

In November 2015, London-based *Al-Fanar Media*, which describes itself as "an editorially independent publication dedicated to covering higher education in the Arab region" reported in a story by Asma' Jawabreh, a freelance reporter and writing fellow at Al-Quds Bard College, that "The conflict between the two major Palestinian political groups—Fatah and Hamas—has turned students against each other at Birzeit University." Furthermore, "Students who belong to the Hamas-affiliated Islamic Wafaa' Bloc student group suffer harassment and worse at the hands of Fatah agents in Birzeit, according to interviews with numerous students at the school, near Ramallah."

The Palestinian Authority, in sometimes violent conflict with Hamas for well over a decade, in 2015 interrogated twenty-five Birzeit University students and detained several over their Hamas affiliation or their criticism of the PA. One student claimed to have been beaten and tortured while in custody. A PA intelligence service officer countered: "We only arrest people who try to create chaos or threaten the stability of the West Bank, whether he belongs to the Islamic bloc or not." He continued, making claims that require more nuanced, less absolute, distinctions, "the [PA] intelligence service watches every Palestinian. That's part of its job. But they have never arrested any students because of their work with the Islamic Bloc. We believe in democracy and pluralism" (Jawabreh).

As Jihad Abaza reported in Egypt's *Daily News* in May 2015, interrogations and detentions by the Palestinian Authority increased after Hamas student groups at Birzeit won a majority of the student council seats in an April election. PA assaults on Hamas student leaders initiated then continue to the present day, with some students supportive of Fatah, the PA's political party, reportedly informing the PA about student activities supportive of Hamas. The ambiguities inherent in such police actions are apparent in the comments a spokesperson for the PA Security Services offered: "We never arrest people for their speech or for their political affiliations," Adnan Al-Dimiri said, "these people have been arrested for the criminal charge of incitement of sectarian violence and other criminal charges." Yet students had been interrogated or arrested in both 2014 and 2015 after they wrote Facebook posts critical of the PA. One resulting charge: "insulting public authorities."

There is some evidence that the PA security forces have recently made a more intensive effort to suppress Hamas on campus. The April 2019 student council elections at Hebron University saw a serious decline in Hamas support; Fatah won thirty seats and Hamas won only 11. Gaza political scientist Adnan Abu Amer claims "These elections were accompanied and preceded by campaigns of repression, persecution, intimidation, and political detention, as well as threats to a large number of university students and their families" ("How Hamas"). He calls it "a serious indicator of the deterioration of the reality of student freedoms in the West Bank." What is clear is that the PA was willing to enter and establish an intimidating presence at Hebron University and on other campuses in the leadup to the election.

Indeed, there are frequent news reports of PA security forces firing weapons into the air on West Bank campuses. Amer fairly includes those weapons discharges as part of the continuing "militarization of student competitions." A September 2019 news story by *Middle East Monitor*, for example, opens with "Four of Birzeit University's student leaders in the occupied West Bank have disappeared after being chased and shot at by Palestinian Authority security officers," the shots, as is regularly the case, most likely having been fired in the air. The story continues with "the PA public intelligence agency broke into the home of one of the Islamic Bloc leaders and confiscated papers, posters, and documents related to the election campaign."

Human Rights Watch and Scholars at Risk, both based in New York, earlier denounced the PA's practices. Along with various news outlets, Scholars at Risk reported in *Academic Freedom Monitor* on several student detentions and beatings by the PA, among them this account of events in 2015: "On April 25, architecture student and current student representative Jihad Salim was allegedly forced into an unmarked vehicle in front of the Birzeit campus and taken to a preventative security office where he was beaten and held for 24 hours, during which he was interrogated about the elections, denied food and water, and forced to remain in physically strenuous positions." A few days earlier, IMEMC news published this report on an April 8 abduction:

A group of human rights organizations have condemned the recent attack on student Musa Dweikat, and his abduction, in front of the campus of An-Najah University, by members of Palestinian intelligence, and calls for an end to similar cases of kidnapping off the streets and arbitrary arrests . . . . According to video footage, two people dressed in civilian clothes, one carrying a pistol, blocked his way while he was passing by Al-Najah University. They then beat him with batons before three other security members riding in a Hyundai microbus joined them. They handcuffed and shoved him inside the car leading him to an unknown destination.

Scholars at Risk's conclusions are uncompromising:

Scholars at Risk is concerned about the arrest, detention, and reported custodial abuse of university students and graduates, apparently as a result of student elections and nonviolent expression and association—conduct which is expressly protected under international human rights instruments including the Universal Declaration of Human Rights. State officials have a responsibility not to interfere with freedom of expression and association, so long as such rights are exercised peacefully and responsibly. Arrest, detention, and abuse aimed at limiting student expression and association undermine academic freedom and related values such as university autonomy.

Human Rights Watch argues fancifully that Hamas "has a large political wing, involvement in which does not amount to incitement to violence," but the distinction is a myth. As Matthew Levitt documents in great detail in *Hamas: Politics, Charity, and Terrorism in the Service of Jihad,*

> Hamas relies on its political and social activists and organizations to build grassroot support for the movement, to spot and recruit future operatives, to provide day jobs and cover to current operatives, and to serve as the logistical and financial support network for the group's terror cells. Often the Hamas operatives running the group's political and charitable offices are closely tied to the group's terror cells, or are themselves current or former terror-cell members." (2)

This means that thorough surveillance of all Hamas activities is necessary. I believe it is important for groups like Human Rights Watch to apply a universal human rights standard to treatment of all people, including students, who are detained and interrogated, but that standard cannot bar the PA from monitoring all Hamas social and political activity and questioning those involved. On the other hand, surveillance and torture are not the same, and the PA engages in both.

Affronts to academic freedom are not limited to PA treatment of students or faculty loyal to Hamas. Islamist students themselves are quite willing to threaten faculty who do not share their religious and cultural views. In July 2012, Scott Jaschik reported in *Inside Higher Education* about the case of Birzeit University cultural studies professor Musa Budeiri, who ran afoul of student ideology when he posted what they considered to be offensive cartoons on his office door: "The cartoons in question are a couple of pages from Superman comics," he explained. "A blogger from the Emirates had taken a few pages from the comics, added a beard to Superman and declared him Islamic Superman, and posted on the Internet. He also erased the English blurb and inserted words of his own in Arabic. In the first, Superman is lying in bed with a woman and she asks him if he is going to marry her; he responds by saying that on the planet Krypton, they are 'not allowed to take a fifth wife.'"

Students distributed a leaflet declaring the cartoons an affront to Islam. The university removed the cartoons and asked the professor to apologize, which he refused to do. He issued a statement pointing out that people should not assume they understood what his intentions were in posting the images. That did not deter the students from issuing threats of physical violence against him, and the university then announced that the nineteen-year veteran would not be returning to teach, an action designed to appease the radical Islamists in the student body. Birzeit meanwhile was reluctant to punish the students involved in threatening violence. The Middle East Studies Association of North America issued a letter declaring that "the actions of the university administration to date risk establishing a dangerous precedent that privileges those who resort to intimidation and violence to contest the freedom of expression" (Mesa "Controversy"). Though it would have been more responsible to acknowledge that the utility of threats of violence was already well-established there.

The protests and threats against Budeiri recall the attacks against Danish cartoonist Kurt Westergaard after he published a series of twelve cartoons featuring the prophet Mohammed. The cartoon that Muslims worldwide objected to most violently was one depicting Mohammed wearing a bomb in his turban (Watt). In 2008 the Danish security services arrested three Muslims for plotting to murder Westergaard, and in 2011 he escaped an attempted murder at his home. To read about Budeiri now is of course to recall the horrific murders of members of the *Charlie Hebdo* staff in Paris on January 7, 2015. There too the offense was the publication of a satirical cartoon featuring Mohammed. Both the threats against Budeiri and the chilling effect of Birzeit's failure to defend his academic freedom are characteristic of an impulse toward appeasing religious intolerance.

In May 2017, Hamas won the student elections at Birzeit for the third straight time, with Hamas's al-Wafaa Islamic Bloc winning 25 seats with a total of 3,778 votes, followed by Fatah's Martyr Yasser Arafat Bloc, which won 22 seats with 3,340 votes. The turnout was 74 percent (Ghorbiah). In May 2018 Hamas was victorious once again with a one-seat margin (Daragmi). The following year's vote was evenly split (Fig. 2). These close votes guarantee that the contests between Fatah and Hamas will remain contentious and that the student body will remain polarized save for those moments when they can unite against a common enemy, whether Israel or their own administration.

6. THE ASSAULTS ON COLLABORATORS AND NORMALIZERS

s the earlier reference to the 1938 murder of Mohammed Dajani's relative Hassan Sidiqui Dajani suggests, the history of Arabs and Palestinians killing their own people for real or imaginary "collaboration" with Israel goes back a good part of a hundred years, often facilitated by authorities failing to pursue such cases. Because I am concerned here with the impact on academic freedom, I am segregating examples of assaults on academics, but that is partly artificial and misleading. It is relevant because it shows there is no special Palestinian exception for academic freedom that would protect faculty from retribution for their political views. Persecution for political dissent is an equal opportunity consequence. But assaults on academics are not alone in creating a climate of intimidation and genuine risk for Palestinian faculty both in Gaza and the West Bank. Beatings as reprisals for the expression of unacceptable political views or participation in joint Israeli-Palestinian projects are far too common to make it into the news. One is mostly left to track assassination attempts or actual murders.

West Bank faculty remember very clearly the murders of Palestinians suspected of collaboration by their fellow Palestinians during the intifadas. According to Peter Beaumont, reporting in the consistently left *Guardian*, "more than 800 suspected collaborators were killed by fellow Palestinians" from 1987-93. Even B'Tselem, the Israeli human rights organization that concentrates overwhelmingly on Israeli violations, reported the murder of nine suspected Palestinian collaborators in 2000-2001. B'Tselem's January 2011 report "Harm to Palestinians suspected of collaborating with Israel" opens with this passage:

> Since the beginning of the al-Aqsa intifada, Palestinians have killed dozens of Palestinian civilians on suspicion of collaboration with Israel. Some of the victims were killed in assassinations conducted by organizations; others died at the hands of Palestinian Authority security forces as a result of being tortured or when attempting to escape, while still others were lynched by crowds of people. Also, the Palestinian Authority killed several Palestinians whom the State Security Court, in a patently unfair judicial process, had convicted of collaborating with Israel.

Regarding the First Intifada, the report observes that "the definition of 'collaboration' was much broader then, and included, for example, directly assisting Israeli security forces by gathering information and trapping wanted persons, serving on Israel's behalf in political positions in local authorities, the Civil Administration, and the Israel Police Force, brokering and selling land to Israeli organizations, failing to participate in work strikes, marketing banned Israeli merchandise." A subsequent passage reads "In many cases, the attacks against suspected collaborators were particularly brutal. Some suspects were abducted, tortured, killed, and then had their bodies mutilated and placed on public display." Amos Harel and Amira Hass reported on the murder of twelve suspected collaborators in West Bank towns in 2002. During 2014's Operation Protective Edge, Hamas was particularly ruthless in killing suspected collaborators. Elhana Miller reports thirty killed in Gaza in July of that year. The title of a 2015 *Daily Mail* article by Larisa Brown and Flora Drury is "Hamas executed Palestinian 'collaborators' with AK-47s in front of hundreds of spectators including children for 'assisting Israel' during last Gaza conflict, reveals Amnesty International."[26] In December 2018, Hamas sentenced six Palestinians to death, one in absentia, for allegedly collaborating with Israel (Rasgon).

---

26. In *Gaza: An Inquest Into Its Martyrdom*, Norman Finkelstein mounts an unsavory defense of the murder of Gazans accused of collaboration with Israel by recalling that "Russian revolutionist Leon Trotsky cogently argued that in the midst of a foreign invasion, the threat of incarceration will not deter potential

Among the deluge of news stories about the killings of suspected collaborators by Palestinians, stories that continue to the present day, therefore, are both accounts of individual incidents and more comprehensive reports. To speak of a "chilling effect," the term routinely used in the West, is completely inadequate. There is an omnipresent sense of clear and present danger. Because academics speak before classes and groups of colleagues, their speech is more exposed than that of many other residents. Mohammed Dajani notably was accused of being a normalizer, not a collaborator. A normalizer would ordinarily regularize normal working relations and communications between Israelis and Palestinians, thereby treating Israel as an acceptable society and its government as one among many worthy of respect, as opposed to a rogue state worthy only of hostility. A collaborator would be a Palestinian actively seeking to advance Israeli interests and thereby supposedly betraying his or her own people. The two categories are essentially interchangeable in some Palestinian quarters, and Palestinians can put their lives in danger by being subject to either accusation. In the West, the BDS movement mostly limits itself to non-violent anti-normalization campaigns, though it aggressively interrupts pro-Israeli speakers and pursues verbal and administrative assaults on Zionist students and faculty. On the West Bank, where BDS is not in control of these campaigns, normalization and collaboration are basically two sides of the same coin and both can have lethal consequences.

In 2016 I was part of a group that met with the director of an Israeli NGO that trains young Israeli and Palestinian professionals in negotiation techniques, with the aim of developing a cadre of nongovernmental professionals who could play a role as skilled negotiators in the event of a revived peace process. Fifteen young people from each side are accepted into a year-long program whose final session takes place in a house on a frigid island off the Swedish coast in mid-winter. It is the only building there, which guarantees isolation and complete

---

collaborators." He proceeds to pose what he calls "the inescapable question, *How else was Hamas supposed to deter collaborators?* [Finkelstein's italics]." This is part of Finkelstein's critique of a UN Human Rights Council report on 2014's Operation Protective Edge. He adds sardonically: "Was Hamas legally required to organize a Collaborator Pride parade" (323)?

concentration on the task. The task is to negotiate a peace treaty, with Palestinians representing the Israeli position and Israelis representing Palestinians. There was one condition for our meeting: we could not name the NGO afterwards. The organization remains confidential to protect the Palestinians from violent reprisals. They would be accused of being collaborators trying to normalize relations with Israel. Nusseibeh and Dajani survived such assaults, but others did not.

7. FREEDOM OF THE PRESS
AND ACADEMIC FREEDOM

Lessons from the assaults on purported collaborators and normalizers are not the only messages about the strict limits to politically acceptable speech that Palestinian faculty in Gaza and the West Bank must receive and internalize. Of the several kinds of freedom of expression and assembly that intersect with or influence academic freedom, probably none is more direct or dispositive than freedom of the press. Some faculty members of course write letters to the editor and op-eds expressing their opinions on public issues. Faculty members in journalism often double as reporters and certainly train students in that field. Faculty in many other fields write accessible reports of their research for publication in popular newspapers or magazines.

More broadly still, faculty members address student audiences for which confidentiality is neither mandated nor expected. The options and consequences for—and the limits to—freedom of the press to a significant degree set the parameters of what it is acceptable and not acceptable for faculty members to say in performing their own professional responsibilities. In a society with a free press that honors academic freedom, the dynamic relationship between the press and academia can seem relatively unproblematic. In a country or territory where some opinions are considered unacceptable affronts to the relevant political powers or to prevailing cultural, moral, or religious values, faculty members will often self-censor contrary views, especially if actual physical assault is the likely consequence of expressing them. Israel within its pre-1967 borders has a free press, but Gaza and the West Bank do not.

1. On November 20, 1996, hooded and armed Hamas militants at an An-Najah University campus rally dedicated to condemning peace agreements signed by Arafat and the Israelis.

2. Birzeit University students supporting Fatah at an April 2019 campus student council election rally.

3. Palestinian students visit a pro-Hamas exhibition at An-Najah University on January 28, 2002, during the Second Intifada. In the large mural, an armed militant wearing a hand grenade offers a symbolic helping hand to struggling Palestinians. The text on the Arabic headband on the figure in the large mural is the first sentence of the Shahada or Islamic creed: "There is no deity but God (Allah)," making him an avatar of jihad, perhaps usurping the agency in the second passage of the Shahada, which is not on the headband: "Muhammad is the messenger of God." Above the table at the bottom are photos of four terrorists (martyrs or *shaheeds*) killed in an IDF raid in Nablus a few days earlier: Karim Mafarjeh (farthest left), Youssef Surabgi, Jasser Samaro, and Nassim al Russ. Samaro and al Russ had built bombs used at the Sbarro pizzeria in Jerusalem and the Dolphinarium in Tel Aviv.

4. Wall mural celebrating Hamas political wing leader Khaled Meshaal (left) and co-founder Sheikh Ahmed Yassin (right) (1937-2004) painted by students at Islamic University of Gaza. Yassin opposed the peace process, the existence of Israel, and promoted armed resistance against the Jewish state. The map on the right represents Israel as an Islamic state. The white dove of peace is framed by its Islamist enabling conditions: armed resistance and religious transformation. The photo is from January 2018.

5. A Birzeit University student uses a sling shot to hurl a rock at Israeli soldiers on March 7, 2019.

6. A Birzeit University student hurls a Molotov cocktail at Israeli soldiers during a November 17, 2012, demonstration against the ongoing Gaza strip offensive.

7. The contemporary logo of Shabiba, the student branch of Fatah at An-Najah University (above) and Birzeit University (below) features a map of Israel transformed into an arm topped by a clenched fist. The aspirational and revolutionary message is clear: a Palestinian state will encompass all of Israel proper. The inclusion of the Dome of the Rock (An-Najah, above right) and the Koran (Birzeit, bottom) adds a religious imperative to the message. The An-Najah logo is topped by the text "From the sea of blood of the Martyrs (Shahids) we will create a state." At the bottom it reads "Student Shabiba Movement * National An-Najah University." Birzeit's logo includes the text "We are returning," invoking the Palestinian goal of returning to pre-1967 Israel and suggesting it is already in progress.

8. Palestinian students visiting a September 2001 An-Najah University re-enactment of the Sbarro pizza restaurant suicide bombing (source: Camera; Matzav). The exhibit included replicas of body parts.
The sign reads "Kosher" in Hebrew, which serves as a sardonic commentary on the re-enactment.

9. A large mural celebrating the Sbarro bombing and promoting the An-Najah re-enactment (source: Little Green Footballs)

10-11. An-Najah exhibits celebrating mockups of a recent stabbing attack (above) and a car ramming (below). A body is atop a blood-soaked sheet (below a blue car) in the lower image. These two photos of violent re-enactments are from the An-Najah Islamic Bloc's Facebook page on March 5, 2015, reprinted by the Meir Amit Intelligence and Terrorism Information Center.

12. Palestinian religious leaders pose in front of a 2015 Al-Quds University Abu Dis campus Christmas tree featuring pictures of Palestinian martyrs. YouTube/Al-Quds Educational Television (Gancman)

13. Hamas protest including mock missiles at Al-Quds University in 2014. Source: Facebook.

As Freedom House reported in 2016, Israel "enjoys a lively, pluralistic media environment . . . . Legal protections for freedom of the press are robust . . . . the Supreme Court has affirmed that freedom of expression is an essential component of human dignity. The legal standing of press freedom has also been reinforced by court rulings that cite principles laid out in Israel's Declaration of Independence." The courts also protect the confidentiality of journalistic sources. It is prohibited, however, to praise violence in print. There are more than a dozen daily newspapers, and most Israelis have cable, satellite, or digital access to international TV.[27]

Press rights in Gaza and the West Bank, in contrast, have been severely constrained, respectively, by Hamas and the Palestinian Authority since Hamas took control of Gaza in 2007. "Under such circumstances, Palestinian journalists have little opportunity to carry out independent reporting, even if they are not affiliated to either Fatah or Hamas" (Gunther). The PA and Hamas fund four of five major Palestinian newspapers; they are not editorially independent. The hostility between the two groups means that they actively suppress each other's media outlets and reporters in the territory they control. In August 2017 Amnesty International reported that Hamas and the PA "have launched a repressive clampdown on freedom of expression over recent months" and that "the detention of journalists was used as a bargaining chip in the rivalry between Fatah and Hamas." As Amnesty's Deputy Middle East and North Africa director Magdalena Mughrabi observed, "By rounding up journalists and shutting down opposition websites the Palestinian authorities in the West Bank and the Gaza Strip appear to be using police state tactics to silence critical media and arbitrarily block people's access to information" ("Palestine: Dangerous escalation").

In Gaza, Fatah-affiliated journalists are frequently detained and assaulted. In the West Bank, restrictions are permitted if press activity threatens "national unity" or "Palestinian values," remarkably vague conditions that virtually mandate self-censorship both for the press and

---

27. Diversity of press opinion in Israel is being compromised by the popularity of the free newspaper *Israel Hayom*, which is owned and subsidized by US casino billionaire Sheldon Adelson, who launched the paper in 2007.

for faculty members who wish to avoid arrest or sanctions. Amnesty
International points out that "the legislation is not sufficiently precise
to allow an individual to regulate conduct accordingly." It is typical of
authoritarian cultures that the restraints on individual speech are so
unpredictable, variable, and threatening that only comprehensive self-
censorship can have a chance of guaranteeing personal safety. "In 2015,
Mada, the Center for Development and Media Freedom in Ramallah,
already found that 80 percent of Palestinian journalists censor themselves and feel they cannot write what they want" (Schneider). "Some
of these journalists are acting out of fear of being arrested, harassed or
losing their jobs. Others might self-censor out of ideology . . . . Those
journalists probably see themselves as foot soldiers in the Palestinian
national struggle" (Toameh "Black Day").

As Freedom House concluded in 2019, "The PA governs in an
authoritarian manner, engaging in acts of repression against journalists
and human rights activists who present critical views on its rule" ("West
Bank"). Defamation under the PA is a criminal offense, and journalists
have been prosecuted for publishing criticism of PA officials. The PA's
"2017 Electronic Crimes Law criminalizes expression aimed at harm-
ing moral and religious values without defining those values, allowing
for arbitrary enforcement . . . . New details on the PA's detention and
harassment of individuals based on their online activity were reported
in 2018, and evidence emerged that the PA has engaged in extensive electronic surveillance of lawyers, activists, political figures, and
others," categories that clearly include students and faculty. Amnesty
International points out that "the new law is being used as a tool to
silence dissenting voices and opposition in the ongoing conflict between
the administrations of the West Bank and Gaza."[28] Journalists have also
been interrogated and detained at Israeli checkpoints.

---

28. Amnesty International's "State of Palestine: Alarming attack on Freedom
of Expression" provides a detailed analysis and critique of the law, which was
adopted by Palestinian President Mahmoud Abbas by presidential decree in
July 2017. Amnesty concludes that "it violates international law and the State
of Palestine's obligations to protect the right to freedom of expression and the
right to privacy." It "permits the arbitrary detention of anyone critical of the
authorities online" and "criminalizes dissent in the cyber sphere," provisions that

One application of the new law has been particularly significant. As Khaled Abu Toameh writes,

> On October 17, 2019, the Palestinian Magistrate Court in Ramallah ordered local internet providers to block access to 59 news websites in accordance with a request from the Palestinian attorney general's office. The order was issued under the Palestinian Cybercrime Law, which allows authorities to direct internet service providers to block websites that allegedly threaten national security, civil peace, public order, or public morals. ("Black Day")

It was a six-month directive, set to expire on April 16, 2020, but that date passed without the ban being lifted. The Palestinian Journalists Syndicate, The Palestinian Center for Development and Media Freedom, and the Palestinian Independent Commission for Human Rights were among the groups calling for the ban to be lifted, all without success.

---

threaten reporters, faculty members, and others. "Article 51 of the law provides for imprisonment and up to 15 years of hard labor in the event a crime online is committed for the purpose of 'disturbing public order,' 'national unity,' 'social peace,' or 'contempt of religion.'" Article 7 would "punish whistle-blowers and journalists who use leaked information."

8. TERRORISM AT AN-NAJAH UNIVERSITY IN NABLUS

The single most disturbing fact about Palestinian higher education is that many Palestinian universities have substantial histories of student involvement in terrorism. Moreover, the size of the network of students involved in terrorism considerably exceeds the number of those who actually execute bombings and end up with their names in the news. Someone has to recruit participants; someone has to persuade them to maintain their commitment; someone has to purchase the bomb components or obtain them in another way; someone has to store the explosives; someone has to manufacture the bombs; someone has to hide them; someone has to scout the target location and evaluate the risk of exposure; someone has to plan the attack and plan the escape route for those intended to survive the attack; someone has to transport the bomber to the site; someone has to create the public announcements that may follow an attack. Consider the infrastructure of the March 27, 2002, Park Hotel bombing that killed thirty innocent civilians:

For example, Muhammad Shrim was head of Kutla Islamiya activists at Khaduri College, a branch of al-Najah University. Shrim was recruited into Hamas's military wing by Amer Khedeiri, a Hamas operative responsible for Kutla Islamiya activities at several schools, including Shrim's Khaduri College. Shrim assisted in the Park Hotel attack in various ways: he obtained video cameras to record the bomber's will, prepared martyr posters, and supplied the suicide bomber's driver with a counterfeit Israeli identification card and instructions for purchasing a car with an Israeli license to transport the attacker on the day of the operation. Though Shrim turned down an invitation to be a suicide bomber, he agreed to provide logistics for other operations. He provided Hamas a safehouse in Tulkarm and established a military cell there tasked with carrying out shooting attacks. Ultimately, Shrim was sentenced to twenty-nine consecutive life sentences and twenty years in prison for his role in the Park Hotel bombing. (Chosak)

The indoctrination process for martyrs can take months, even years. A still larger community of students and faculty may participate in publicizing and celebrating the attack, and those public celebrations assist in recruitment of the next generation of terrorists.

Calibrating the degree to which each of the various forms of Palestinian campus anti-Zionism—from face-to-face recruitment of individuals to paramilitary and terrorist groups, to anti-Zionist and anti-Semitic courses, to internet and social media dissemination of hate rhetoric, to public events that celebrate terrorist violence and martyred heroes (Figs. 1, 3, 4, 8, 9, 10, 11, 12, 13), to campus assaults on students and faculty which normalize violence—will require more intricate study than can be accomplished now. Much of it will have to come from Palestinians themselves.

The largest Palestinian university, An-Najah University in Nablus in the northern area of the West Bank, appears to have had the largest number of actual suicide bombers, along with a series of particularly aggressive public events endorsing lethal anti-Jewish violence (Levitt "Teaching Terror") (Figs. 1, 3, 13). The university's history began with the establishment of an elementary school in 1918. At the time Nablus was a heavily Muslim market town. The elementary school evolved into a teacher training institute in 1965 and became a liberal arts college chartered as a university in 1977. The surrounding community helped give the college an Islamic and nationalist character that it retains today.

One notorious cultural event at An-Najah, an event that doubles as indirect recruitment activity, was the September 2001 Second Intifada commemorative exhibition. The exhibit celebrated the August 2001 suicide bombing that killed 15 people, among them two Americans, and wounded 130 others at Jerusalem's Sbarro Pizza (Meir Amit) (Figs. 8, 9). The young woman who "transported the 10 kilogram nail-enhanced bomb, handed it to Izzedin Al-Masri, and escorted him through Jerusalem's city center to Sbarro restaurant, the target she had chosen for its crowd of women and children" and who "instructed 'her weapon,' Al-Masri, the suicide bomber, to delay his detonation until she had time to escape the scene" was Birzeit University student Ahlam Ahmad al-Tamimi (Horovitz). She was recruited by Hamas. Prior to Sbarro, she had planted a device in the basement supermarket of Jerusalem's Hamashbir department store on King George St., but the bomb was poorly constructed and went off without any casualties.[29] As of 2020, the FBI is seeking al-Tamimi's extradition from Jordan. As Miriam Elman reminds us, Tamimi has publicly celebrated her role in the bombing ("Never Forget").

Sponsored by students supporting Hamas, the An-Najah exhibit's main attraction was a room-sized installation including shattered furniture spattered with fake blood and human body parts. The exhibit also included a large rock in front of a mannequin dressed in the black hat, jacket, and trousers often worn by ultra-Orthodox Jews. Drawing on a Hadith[30] universally known to Palestinians, a recording from inside the rock announces: "O believer, there is a Jewish man behind me. Come and kill him." Dissemination of this Hadith (no. 2921) is a shorthand way of signaling a religious warrant for killing Jews, just as it gives a theological basis for opposition to the Jewish state and eliminates any distinction between Jews and Israelis. It is easy, as I have,

---

29. Tamimi was captured, convicted, and sentenced to 16 life terms, but then released as part of the prisoner exchange that freed Israeli soldier Gilad Shalit in 2011. Born in Jordan, al-Tamimi was returned there after her release. Horovitz's essay covers the effects of the bombing on the family of Maliki Roth, who was among those killed in the bombing. There is a continuing effort to extradite her to face trial for the death of two Americans in the Sbarro bombing. She is on the FBI's Most Wanted List.

30. Separate from the Quran, which Muslims regard as the word of God, Hadith are a body of statements and actions attributed to the prophet Muhammed. Much of Islamic law (Sharia) is derived from Hadith, rather than the Quran.

to encounter Palestinians hostile to Israel who quote the Hadith from memory. Efforts to explain away the stark message endorsing murder it communicates ring hollow. Thus Ulvi Karagedik of the University of Vienna's Department for Islamic Theological Studies tells us "as it contains fictitious elements, such as prophecies and speaking stones, it has no connection with the everyday life of Muslims and cannot be transferred to the present" (43). A few pages earlier, however, Karagedik reminded us that the Hadith "are generally accepted by Muslims as part of their religious truth . . . and play an important role in their everyday life," constituting "an integral part of Muslim reality" (36). Suffice it to say that efforts to discount the power of the prophetic and the symbolic among religious communities present insurmountable challenges.

The exhibit embodied a certain blood lust, but it also reflected a version of Islamist contempt for Jews. That was reinforced by a cartoon version of the Hadith in the exhibit, certainly not the only caricature portrait of the Hadith to be found among Palestinians. At least three Palestinian schools post a more intricate version of the cartoon on their Facebook pages (Marcus 21).[31] In this case, a wide-eyed Jew with braided hair hides behind a cartoon tree at night, clutching its trunk, which reaches up into a flat pale green canopy. It may be that these popular celebrations of Hadith 2921 undercut the sense that the murder of Jews is a sacred duty. Killing Jews becomes instead an object of vulgar popular celebration, a call to murder horrifically trivialized. This kind

---

31. Marcus et al detail the many Palestinian elementary and secondary schools named after terrorists and describe the impact this and other practices have on Palestinian children. They also give examples of yet another way Palestinian universities honor terrorism—by naming tournaments and athletic events in their honor (25). "Al-Quds University honored Hamas terrorist Ibrahim Al-Akari, just four days after his terror attack in Jerusalem on Nov. 5, 2014, killing two and injuring at least 13" by co-sponsoring the Martyr Ibrahim Al-Akari Tournament. "The Al-Quds University Institute of Modern Media named teams in a tournament after a series of terrorists, including Yahya Ayyash, the first Hamas suicide bomb builder and planner, known as 'the Engineer.' He is considered the founder of Palestinian suicide terror, and was behind attacks killing dozens of Israelis and injuring hundreds. Another team was named after Dalal Mughrabi, who, as mentioned, led the most lethal terror attack in Israel's history, [which] killed 37 civilians, 12 of them children."

of material "dehumanizes victims, making it psychologically easier for would-be terrorists to fantasise, plan and commit attacks" (Community Security Trust, 7).

Yasser Arafat eventually shut the exhibition down. Some US universities would likely regard it as protected, if deplorable, political expression. However, it is unlikely it would, at least initially, survive a policy prohibiting explicit anti-Semitism on campus like the one the University of California Regents adopted in 2016 if it included enforcement mechanisms. If such an exhibition were to be removed by the administration at a public university in the US, one could well imagine Palestine Legal or the ACLU contesting the action on constitutional grounds and prevailing. Indeed, unlikely but possible would be a pro-Israel campus group incorporating some of the same material into an exhibition highlighting evidence of anti-Semitism on the West Bank. The bottom line is that the exhibit should be allowed in the US but vigorously condemned and used as a teachable moment. As a three-dimensional embodiment of extreme anti-Semitic speech, it would be exceptionally painful to Jewish students, though there are campus constituencies that would not be troubled by that fact. In the Middle East generally, and certainly in Palestine, however, one confronts a different reality. As I argued earlier, deciding what constitutes incitement to violence often has to be a contextual, culturally specific process. On the West Bank this exhibition plausibly constituted incitement to lethal violence.

The 2001 exhibition was not the last such installation at An-Najah. Most dramatically, the Islamic Bloc at An-Najah staged a March 2015 exhibit on Jerusalem that celebrated stabbing and ramming attacks and other acts of violence against Jews (Figs. 10, 11). The Islamic Bloc's Facebook page included a photograph of the most provocative display: a full-sized mock-up of a car driving over the body of an Israeli civilian, possibly a settler. Beneath him is a white sheet soaked in blood. Among those attending the opening ceremony was the Dean of Najah's Faculty of Engineering who sported a green Hamas scarf. A year earlier the Islamic Bloc's "Promise and Loyalty" exhibit for Shahids' (Martyrs') Week featured a photo of a model of a bombed bus headed (in Arabic) "When you see the roof of a bus fly off, know that this is a Hamas operation" (Palestinian Media Watch). In May 2017 students named the graduating class of economics and political science students "The Class of the Bride of the Coast—Martyr Dalal Mughrabi." Mughrabi was among the terrorists who died in the infamous 1978 Coastal Road massacre that killed thirty-eight Israeli civilians, among them thirteen children.

Israeli forensic team gathers evidence from the bus destroyed in the Coastal Road massacre. Photo: IDF Spokesman Unit.

In 2010 six members of the An-Najah University faculty were arrested by Palestinian Authority security forces for being closely linked to a charity that is suspected of being a front for Hamas (Kalman "6 faculty Members"). The unfortunate bottom line in the West Bank context is that there is no fixed line between valid political expression and terrorist recruitment. Should students there or in Israel be permitted to celebrate Nakba Day? Yes. Should the An-Najah exhibit have been closed? Possibly not, even though the Palestinian Authority has been engaged in a lethal struggle with Hamas. Should the An-Najah faculty have been arrested? If the evidence of their involvement with Hamas fundraising was convincing, yes. While it is often difficult enough for a country not at war to protect political expression that is deeply objectionable, it is still more difficult to decide these questions in Israel and in the Palestinian territories.

When students at Birzeit late in 2016 "held a rally on campus, during which they dressed in fatigues, held machines guns, and called to 'blow up' Israelis," should the university have condemned it and prohibited similar events in the future (Frommer)? In the US, though perhaps not in open weapons carry states, the mix of guns and calls to violence would likely be actionable. Imagine adding assault rifles to the August 2017 Charlottesville, Virginia, white nationalist rally with its chants of "The Jews Will Not Replace Us." From an uncompromising free speech perspective, a campus might prohibit armed protests but not the military apparel and the incendiary expression. Matters are complicated, however, when people regularly act on calls for anti-Semitic violence.

We cannot, however, provide an adequate account of Palestinian campus involvement in terrorism unless we not only detail terror-supportive campus environments but also report actual student involvement in violence. We can begin to do so by tracking arrests of current and former college and university students for overt terrorist activity. One way or another, the campus environment at An-Najah and at other institutions for decades has helped prepare some current students for extreme violent activity. Others leave school to join terror cells and some, in effect, make terrorism their career choice, albeit often for careers cut short by imprisonment or death. It is not just deeply troubling but also definitional that many Palestinian universities have substantial histories of student involvement in terrorism.

Although campus violence predates the First Intifada (1987–1991 or 1993), it was in those years that incitement mounted. Incitement intensified during the Second Intifada (2000–2005), and violence escalated. During the Second Intifada, universities were sometimes closed because of specific terrorist activity. As James Bennet writes in the *New York Times* in 2003, "In Hebron, the army closed Hebron University and the Polytechnic Institute, which it said had been used as training grounds for numerous terrorist attacks. The army said that, at the university, leaders of the Islamic fundamentalist group Hamas had used the chemistry lab in the Faculty of Science to train students to make bombs. It said that students had used computers at the Polytechnic Institute to download bomb-making guides from a Hamas Web site." As Matthew Levitt summarized in 2007, campus incitement played out in what amounted to a demonic exercise of academic freedom:

> Hamas propaganda—pamphlets, posters, and myriad other printed collateral—literally litter Palestinian university campuses. For example, a timetable for university lectures at one campus featured pictures of Hamas suicide bombers. During student elections at Birzeit University in 2003, Hamas candidates reenacted suicide bombings by blowing up models of Israeli buses. In one Birzeit campus debate, a Hamas candidate taunted his Fatah challenger by boasting, "Hamas activists in this University killed 135 Zionists. How many did Fatah activists from Birzeit kill?"

The consequences are gruesome. The March 27, 2002, Park Hotel bombing in Netanya killed thirty people; a number of the perpetrators came from Kutla Islamiya (the Islamic Bloc) at Palestinian universities, particularly An-Najah in Nablus. As Jamie Chosak and Julie Sawyer detail in a report from The Washington Institute, "For example, Muhammad Shrim was head of *Kutla Islamiya* activists at Khaduri College, a branch of An-Najah University." As detailed above, he provided documents and logistics for this and other operations. Ali Khudeiri, a Hamas recruiter for the operation, was a former Engineering student at An-Najah. Four days after the Park Hotel attack, a Hamas suicide bomber blew himself up at the Matza restaurant in Haifa, killing fifteen. Qeis Adwan, an An-Najah architectural engineering student and leader of the student union, "masterminded the bombing; he produced the bomb, recruited and dispatched the bomber" (Chosak):

Adwan also found and dispatched the Hamas suicide bomber who perpetrated the August 2001 attack at the Sbarro Pizzeria restaurant in Jerusalem, a bombing that left fifteen people dead, including five children. One month later Adwan dispatched an Israeli-Arab he had personally recruited to perpetrate a suicide attack at a crowded railway station in Nahariya, leaving four dead. Yet Adwan's involvement in terrorism extended beyond recruiting and dispatching bombers. Adwan became a specialist in bomb making for Hamas terrorist activities, manufacturing weapons, explosives, and Qassam rockets. Adwan also coordinated military attacks and financial matters between the West Bank and Gaza Strip for Hamas, and, according to Israeli security services, was "in touch with Hamas headquarters in Jordan and Syria." Adwan had been on Israel's most-wanted list since summer 2001; on April 5, 2002, Israeli forces killed Adwan in a targeted assassination. (Chosak)

Margot Dudkevitch details a cluster of university-related terrorist arrests in the spring and summer of 2004. They include a Hamas squad exposed in July composed almost entirely of An-Najah University students (IMRA). The squad leader was Ala'a Joisi (also transliterated as Alaa' Zuhayr Nimr Jayusi):

Security forces recently foiled a Hamas plot to bomb sites in Netanya, infiltrate a terrorist into a settlement in Samaria, and kidnap a soldier. Details of the plot were released by the Shin Bet on Tuesday, including information about the arrest of four Hamas terrorists, all university students in Nablus and Kalkilya, by security forces in June and July. The affair reveals intensive attempts by Hamas in Nablus to launch attacks. The cell planned to kidnap a soldier and demand the release of Palestinian security prisoners incarcerated in Israel; launch a suicide bombing in a wedding hall or antique shop in the Netanya industrial zone; shoot at one of the Jewish communities located near Kalkilya; and dispatch a terrorist posing as a deaf and mute peddler to infiltrate Shoham and shoot residents. Among those arrested, Ala'a Joisi, 23, originally of Tulkarm, headed the cell and was one of the leaders of the Kutla Islamiya movement at An-Najah University in Nablus. In March, security forces thwarted a suicide car bombing which he masterminded. Joisi was arrested on June

10. Khaled Ahmed Salim, 21, of Jayous in the Kalkilya area, was a member of the Kutla Islamiya movement at the Open University in Kalkilya. Salim was arrested by security forces on June 9. Khir Ahmed Wahdan, 26, of Rantiss in the Binyamin region, also a student at An-Najah and active in the Kutla Islamiya movement, was incarcerated in Israel between 2000-2003 for terrorist activities. Wahdan was arrested on June 15. Osama Rahman Abu Mahane, 23, of Atil, an Israeli identity card holder, also studied at An-Najah and was a member of the Kutla Islamiya movement. Mahane, who worked at an ice cream factory in the Netanya industrial zone, compiled preliminary information in preparation for the planned suicide attack there. He was arrested on July 7. Details regarding six Fatah Tanzim members—including two top commanders—killed by special undercover Border Police units in the streets of Tulkarm on Saturday, were released for publication on Tuesday. Mahdi Tanbuz, the 21-year-old commander of the Tulkarm cell, and his deputy Hani Mahmud Aweideh, 26, were both killed in the gun battle. Tanbuz and Aweideh were recruited to the Tulkarm cells in 2002. According to officials, both were responsible for planning and dispatching numerous shootings and bombings carried out by Tanzim in the Tulkarm area over the past two years. In March, they initiated plans to send a terrorist to infiltrate Avnei Hefetz and shoot at drivers entering and leaving the community. In recent days, Tanbuz was planning a shooting against soldiers deployed in the Tulkarm area. Aweideh was in charge of the cell which launched a shooting at the David Palace banquet hall in Hadera in January 2002 in which six Israelis were murdered. Two others killed were identified as Said Nasser, a 16-year-old a member of the cell run by Tanbuz, and Abed al-Rahim Shadid, 34. Shadid was responsible for the murder of a number of Palestinians he suspected of collaborating with Israeli authorities.

In July as well, "A Fatah/Tanzim squad was exposed in Nablus, directed by Hezbollah (July 2, 2004). Its members, who were arrested in Ramallah, reached Nablus and were on their way to perpetrate a suicide bombing attack in Jerusalem. Guiding the prospective suicide bomber

was Shadi Masoud 'Izzat 'Umar, an An-Najah University student"
(IMRA).

Matthew Levitt in *Hamas: Politics, Charity, and Terrorism in the
Service of Jihad* provides a bullet list of additional bombers who came
out of An-Najah:

- Hasham Najar, who conducted a suicide attack with an explosive
  belt at a restaurant frequented by Israel soldiers and Jewish settlers
  in Mehola on December 22, 2000, wounding three;
- Hamed Abu Hijla, who detonated a car bomb carrying an estimated
  twenty kilograms (forty-four pounds) of explosives in Netanya on
  January 1, 2001, injuring nineteen bystanders;
- Jamal Nasser, who detonated a car bomb next to a school bus on
  April 29, 2001;
- Muayad Salah, who prematurely blew himself up en route to a
  suicide operation on January 8, 2001;
- Asam Reihan, who attacked a bus near Emanuel with a roadside
  bomb and automatic weapons, killing ten and wounding thirty;
- Darin Abu Aisha, who blew herself up at the Makabim checkpoint
  on February 27, 2002, wounding three people;
- Muhammad al-Ghul, who blew himself up on a Jerusalem bus on
  June 18, 2002, killing nineteen and wounding over seventy people.
  (128–129)

In 2005 An-Najah student Amir Hotari and his friends formed a military
cell that produced explosive charges and executed attacks, including one
near his village of Haja, Qalqila. He admitted they planned an attack in
Tel Aviv and a suicide attack elsewhere in Israel. Ivas Ghuri, Ali Shtaya,
Fauzi Kakoura, and Hindawi Kawarik, all An-Najah students, admitted
to planning and executing shooting attacks and to planting explosives
(Israeli Security Agency). A number of An-Najah students were arrested
and brought in for interrogation in 2009 alone.

Meanwhile, both plans for mass killings and attacks on individuals
continue to the present day. Muhammed al-Faqih, a former An-Najah
student who spent four years in prison in punishment for Islamic
Jihad activity in Nablus, completed his studies at Palestine Polytechnic
University as a member of Hamas's military wing, *Izzadin Kassam*. On
July 1, 2016, he shot and killed Otniel Yeshiva director Rabbi Michael

Mark in a drive-by attack that also wounded Mark's wife and children. Faqih was later killed in a battle with police after he refused to surrender (Gili Cohen). On December 1st of the same year, Marem Hassoneh, a twenty-year-old English major at An-Najah, was shot dead when she tried to attack soldiers at a checkpoint with a kitchen knife.

Given this history of terrorist connections, is it a good idea for universities in other countries to establish conventional partnerships with An-Najah, to pretend that it is a university that serves much the same purpose as institutions in Asia, Europe, and the Americas? There are other relationships between American and Palestinian institutions, like that of Bard with Al-Quds, but the most widely criticized agreement is the 2014 Memorandum of Understanding (MOU) between An-Najah and San Francisco State University. Initiated by Nablus-born Rabab Abdulhadi, director of SFSU's Arab and Muslim Ethnicities and Diasporas Initiative, and approved by SFSU's president Leslie Wong, the MOU is designed to promote exchanges and collaborations between the two institutions. The arrangement has been widely debated for years, with petitions circulated in its defense.

From the perspective of this essay, perhaps the most notable claim occurs in the 2017 resolution promoted by the California Faculty Association, which condemns "the unsubstantiated claim . . . that the university [An-Najah] is 'a recruitment facility for terrorism.'" Although An-Najah is not exclusively a terrorist recruitment center, the claim that it is partly one has clearly been substantiated. Nonetheless, academic freedom gives SFSU the right to make An-Najah a sister institution if it so chooses. Academic freedom does not, however, protect Professor Abdulhadi, President Wong, or SFSU from criticism for doing so. Some of the criticism has arguably been vulgar, but the optics of an American university campus with a history of repeated anti-Zionist and anti-Semitic incidents partnering with a Palestinian university that treasures those of its students who have killed Jews are not ennobling. [32] There is

---

32. For an overview of the history and sources of anti-Semitism at SFSU, see Rossman-Benjamin's "Identity Politics, the Pursuit of Social Justice, and the Rise of Campus Antisemitism." As Rossman-Benjamin points out, in 1997 SFSU's president Robert Corrigan himself observed that "San Francisco State is considered the most anti-Semitic campus in the nation."

a real possibility that some fiercely anti-Zionist SFSU faculty members will encourage the worst impulses at An-Najah.

Despite these serious reservations, I would not boycott An-Najah, as I believe conversations between Palestinian and Western faculty and students have some positive potential. But uninformed comprehensive endorsements of the entire institution would be misguided and counterproductive. There are no easy answers to this conundrum. At the very least, however, institutional relationships need to include forthright recognition of the dual character of Palestinian higher education, and collaborations with particular An-Najah programs need to be based on thorough knowledge and Western institutional review of their character. Indeed, some collaborations should be rejected because the programs violate appropriate norms for academic freedom.

9. STUDENT TERRORISTS AT OTHER PALESTINIAN CAMPUSES

An-Najah is far from being alone in contributing students to terrorism. For example, Salem Sultan, a student of electronics at Hebron Polytechnic, helped produced Bangalore torpedoes and other explosives. Gaser Wahdan of the Kaduri College in Tul Karm hurled Molotov cocktails at IDF troops. Particularly chilling is the story of Fatah military wing Tanzim member and Abu Dis University student Tayoun Tayoun. Dr. Daniel Yaakobi of Yakir in the northern West Bank brought his car to Tayoun's brother Ahmed's garage in the village of Haja for repair on July 27, 2006. As Yaakobi exited his vehicle, Tayoun struck him over the head with a wrench and continued beating him with a stick until he collapsed and died. Soon two friends, Amar Nofel and Nassim Gabit, arrived and helped Tayoun with the body. They stuffed the body in the car trunk, then drove the car away and burned it to cover up the murder. The investigation was completed and arrests were made in 2009.[33] (Israel Security Agency; The Yeshiva World; Miskin).

As Hamas tactics have shifted more recently, student participation in active terror cells has intensified again. Moreover, as Avi Issacharoff

---

33. Tayoun Tayoun confessed to the murder during a Shin Bet interrogation and said it had been retaliation for the murder of Islamic Jihad operative Hamada Shtiwi, who was killed by security forces one day earlier. Shtiwi was suspected of planning to smuggle a suicide bomber into Israel. Tayoun received life imprisonment.

writes, "Today's terrorists have no desire for an on-the-run lifestyle; they want to commit the attack and get away with it—and to go back to their jobs, their regular lives." He adds that "terror cells are now frequently being established without affiliation to a Palestinian group, but rather on the basis of introductions between friends, fellow university students and/or connections on social networks. Such cells are exceptionally hard for the security services to penetrate" (Issacharoff "Israel foiled").

Hamas, nonetheless, continues to organize its own terror cells. In December 2015, as Gili Cohen, Judah Ari Gross, and Avi Issacharoff each report separately, Israeli Defense Forces reported uncovering and arresting members of a Hamas terror cell in Abu Dis near Jerusalem. Many of the operatives were students at Al-Quds University, a Palestinian institution of about 14,000 students with campuses in Jerusalem, Abu Dis, and al-Bireh (near Ramallah). The authorities involved reported that the group planned suicide attacks in Israel, with some trained by Hamas to manufacture explosive devices and suicide belts. There was particular interest in recruiting students who held Israeli citizenship, as they could move around the country more freely. One Ahmed Jamal Musa Azzam, aged 24, from Qalqilya, "was instructed to recruit fellow students at Al-Quds University in order to buy materials for explosives, rent spaces for the terror ring, and recruit people to carry out attacks," and he succeeded in doing so (Gili Cohen). Those students are named in news stories. The Israeli Defense Forces reported that an explosives lab was found in Azzam's apartment in Abu Dis. As Issacharoff observed, "Had this Abu Dis cell succeeded, it could have changed the entire nature of the current conflict." One or two suicide bombings would have intensified pressure on the IDF to take more aggressive preventive action, and the authority of the PA would have been seriously under-mined. Another terror cell including Al-Quds students was uncovered in Bethlehem. "Several AQU students established an explosive lab in Abu Dis, intending to perpetrate suicide attacks as well as non-suicide bombings" (Levy "Terror Academy"). Funding and instructions came from Hamas in Gaza. "Mohand Halabi, who killed Nahmia Lavi and Aaron Bennett in the current terror wave's first stabbing attack, was a law student at the university" (Levy).

The pattern of Hamas-organized preparations and planning for terror has continued, and it is entirely possible that one or more planned mass bombings of a civilian target will succeed. In March 2018, the Shin Bet reported it had filed charges against three Palestinians, including two Birzeit University students, Issa Shalaida, 21, and Omar Mas'ud, 20, with links to Hamas's military wing in Gaza. They were recruited to Hamas via Facebook to carry out terror attacks and assist with funds transfers (Blumenthal). As Judah Ari Gross reported in an August 2019 story, in June 2019 the Shin Bet arrested members of a Hebron-based terror cell planning a bombing attack in Jerusalem targeting both Israelis and the Palestinian Authority. Several university students were among those arrested, including Tamer Rajah Rajbi, 22, from Hebron's Palestine Polytechnic University. Rajbi, who was active in the Hamas-affiliated al-Kutla al-Islamiya student group, was assisted by fellow student Yusef Atrash, 22, who purchased bomb-making components. In Rajbi's possession was a 6.6-pound bomb with dozens of metal fragments attached, designed to inflict the equivalent of shrapnel wounds on bystanders. Rajbi was building bombs in his home, having been taught by two Hamas operatives from Gaza, Ramzi Alouk and Ahmed Katari. Alouk had earlier been deported to Gaza from the Aida refugee camp near Bethlehem (Kerstein). The camp was peaceful enough when I visited it in 2019, but that may have been a surface perception.

Engagement of Birzeit students in these terror cells has been facilitated over several years by Hamas victories in the student government elections noted earlier (Fig. 13). As Adnan Abu Amer reported in 2016, in an April 2015 student council election at Birzeit, Hamas bested rival Fatah, the Palestinian Authority's political wing, realigning student political allegiances and arguably enhancing campus recruitment opportunities for terrorist activities. Birzeit had long been considered a Fatah stronghold, so the political reversal was significant. In the absence of general elections, some saw the campus vote as a more general indicator of West Bank political sentiment. This cultural and political environment presents serious challenges to both Israel and the Palestinian Authority. Campus politics and political reality in East Jerusalem and the West Bank bear little relationship to what Americans routinely experience in their own country. Impressionable students in

Palestinian universities have the opportunity to escalate from more conventional political advocacy to violent activities that threaten both the campus and the general public.

On March 7, 2018, the student chairman of the Student Council at Birzeit, Omar al-Kiswani, was arrested on campus and brought in for questioning by the Shin Bet, the IDF, and the police in connection with his receipt of 150,000 Euros to be used in Hamas organizing efforts. Kiswani had been detained by the Palestinian Authority after Hamas won the Student Council election in 2015, so he had already drawn the attention of the security services (Sneineh). Kiswani's 2018 arrest reflected continuing terror cell organizing among Birzeit students. "In 2017 a Hamas cell led by members located in the Gaza Strip, recruited students at Birzeit University to carry out suicide attacks" (Ahronheim). A Shin Bet statement pointed out that "This is another expression of the efforts of the Hamas headquarters in Turkey and the Gaza Strip to accelerate activity in the West Bank. They launder funds and hide them in many locations throughout the West Bank," adding that the exposure and arrest of the two men who studied at Birzeit University "once again points to the great importance that the Hamas headquarters attaches to student activity" (Ahronheim). The University absurdly protested that the Kiswani arrest was "arbitrary" and a violation of international humanitarian law, claiming that the campus was protected from such an intrusion, and MESA (the Middle East Studies Association) sent a letter protesting his "arbitrary" arrest and detention as well, insisting that Israel is required to "protect universities as spaces of education." But many countries would allow the arrest of a student collaborating with a terrorist group to occur anywhere. As A. J. Caschetta writes, "Ignoring the long history of terrorist recruiting on Palestinian campuses and the terrorism committed by Palestinian students under the tutelage of their Hamas and Fatah advisors, MESA falsely portrays Palestinian academics and students as benign."

In March 2020 the Shin Bet security services arrested three Hamas members who were planning attacks at Teddy soccer stadium in Jerusalem and on IDF soldiers near Ramallah, though the stadium proved to be too well guarded (Emerson). The three men had met while studying at Birzeit University; they were members of a student fraternity that is a center of Hamas activity. "The Hamas network among university students there served as a 'go between' for the three Hamas operatives and provided them funds" (JNS "Israel thwarts"). As Steve Emerson, executive director of the Washington, DC-based Investigative Project on Terrorism, writes, "Gaza-based Hamas figures seek out talented students who are motivated and capable of building bombs. The terrorist organization also instructs its recruits to mobilize other students and young Palestinians to form cells in the West Bank. The latest arrests highlight the dangers of Hamas' West Bank terrorist infrastructure, among educational institutions and beyond." The men—Ahmed Sajada (27), Muhammad Hamad (26), and Omar Eid (24) at the time of arrest—were, respectively, from Qalaniya refugee camp, Kafr Aqab near Jerusalem, and the village of Deir Jarir near Ramallah. The three had hoped to use home-made explosives against IDF vehicles and checkpoints. Terrorist organizing continues at Palestinian universities to the present day. It persisted even during the coronavirus pandemic.

What, one may ask, would actually be required to be confident that Palestinian universities were in fact protected "spaces of education," as MESA demands, rather than the dual function institutions they have been for decades and continue to be today—sites at once for education and for the radical militarization of students? MESA knows better when it assigns the responsibility to protect academic freedom to Israel alone and ignores the primary responsibility the PA and universities themselves must take. Are there sufficient numbers of Palestinian faculty members ready to help lead a campaign to demilitarize campuses? Will the student councils aligned with Hamas allow such a movement? Will those who speak out for nonviolence put themselves at risk? How long would it take to reform Palestinian higher education?

The pervasive politicization and militarization of education that took place in Palestinian Universities in the 1980s has left a legacy that is still relevant today. Unless we are willing to include terrorist recruitment as part of a university's educational mission, then the Palestinian universities listed here are clearly not "spaces of education" as the concept is normally understood. Judith Butler would like us to believe that Israeli arrests and detentions in the West Bank amount to examples of how "incarcerated students are denied their freedom to hold political

views that may not be acceptable to the occupying state," but advocating for and organizing on behalf of a terrorist group is not simply
an expression of political opinion, even though students and faculty in
the West can easily be misled into thinking that conventional political
expression is the only issue at stake.

To avoid the mass conflict that ensues when uniformed Israeli forces
arrive on a campus in large numbers, the March 2018 Kiswani arrest
was carried out by a small group in plain clothes (Fulbright). When the
IDF instead arrives in uniform on a Palestinian campus in force, chaos
often results, with paving stones and limestone blocks hurled from one
side of the battlefield and rubber bullets fired in response. Photographs
and digital footage of rubble-strewn buildings flood social media.
The question remains: what can such tactics accomplish? While those
North Americans and Europeans who castigate Israel and the IDF for
their policies and actions are typically unwilling to admit it, Al-Quds,
An-Najah, Birzeit, and other Palestinian campuses, despite the quality
of many of their academic offerings, are fundamentally different kinds
of institutions from those in their own countries. Allying with a Hamas
cell is not the same as joining a chapter of College Democrats or College
Republicans on an American campus. In the West Bank and Gaza, we
are not in Kansas anymore.

Because the threat posed by incitement to violence on Palestinian
university campuses and involvement in terrorism by Palestinian students continues to be real, the challenge to authorities consequently
entails not only transcendent principles like academic freedom but also
the practical question of the tactics best suited to the unique circumstances on the West Bank. In my spring 2016 conversation with him,
Mohammed Dajani was forthright in detailing the political challenges
that both the IDF and the Palestinian Authority face on Palestinian
campuses. Despite rumors to the contrary, however, the IDF is not
likely to find major weapons caches on campus, though it may have
been justified in conducting such searches during the Second Intifada.
And terror cells will recruit on campus but are less likely to meet there.
Dajani argued, persuasively in my view, that the IDF should challenge
student members of these groups in their apartments and off-campus

meeting sites rather than on campus itself. Indeed, the majority of such raids and arrests are conducted off-campus.

2014 An-Najah graduates pose with three fingers. Credit: Eyan Yasin (Israeli Defense Forces)

One of the differences between on-campus and off-campus raids is illustrated by coordinated raids in January 2016: the IDF raided Birzeit University and seized Hamas propaganda and computer equipment from the campus, but simultaneous area raids more significantly located weapons caches. Some campus raids, however, have had specific rationales. In 2014, between June 19–22, Israeli forces raided Birzeit, Al-Quds, the Arab American, and the Palestinian Polytechnic universities, the latter two in Jenin and Hebron respectively. Those raids were part of the desperate search for three Israeli teenagers kidnapped on June 12. Given the long history of university student involvement in violence, it was not unreasonable for the IDF to have thought there might be relevant evidence at one of those locations. At the An-Najah graduation that June, dozens of students posed for a group photograph holding up three fingers to symbolize the three kidnapped teens; the gesture spread quickly throughout the West Bank as a sign of pride in the crime. It seems somewhat oblivious for organizations such as Scholars at Risk to worry that such raids could "call into question, in fact or perception, the neutrality of higher education communities" (2015, 30). The neutrality train left the station years ago.

Unsurprisingly, some university employees also have off-campus terror connections. After a March 2015 arrest of a terror cell, as reported in a US State Department report (IOSAC), it was revealed that "one of the cell's members was employed at Abu Dis University as a cafeteria attendant," hardly a major revelation, but notable as a mundane reminder that these institutions face different challenges than our own. Perhaps the IDF hopes its campus incursions will have a chilling effect on illegal political activity, but the opposite result may well be more probable. Palestinian campuses are not simply innocent academic enclaves assaulted by invading Israeli armies, despite efforts by the BDS movement and credulous Western academics and media to characterize them that way.

A continuing reign of intermittent political terror by Palestinians themselves shapes the psychological environment and eliminates anything like academic freedom for political expression. Yet an IDF incursion is by its nature a blunt instrument, disrupting the activities of all who live in a dorm or study and work on a campus (dormitory incursions are now more common than those in the central campus), not just the smaller number who have crossed a line into illegal activities. An IDF incursion inevitably blurs the distinction between political activity that should be protected by academic freedom and activity that is against the law, though the latter does commonly occur on Palestinian campuses, and it is a considerable challenge to distinguish between legal and illegal political activities when terrorist groups are at issue. The likelihood that campus incursions by the IDF will create broad antagonism is high. Dajani is effectively urging targeted anti-terrorist actions that are more likely to be of practical success.

IDF raids do gather literature distributed on campus, and that is an important part of tracking the character of the incitement to violence taking place there. But such literature will be available in off-campus apartments and elsewhere as well. In addition, confidential informants are able to supply it. One can reasonably expect that the PA security services will also be willing to share Hamas recruitment literature with Israel, assuming that a permanent break in security cooperation does not take place.

While the number of students actually carrying out suicide bombings has always been small, those involved in helping plan them is larger. Added to that violence are those who carry out or facilitate more conventional bombing attacks. Then there is the much larger number of students who endorse and actively advocate for violence against Israelis. All of this, along with faculty advocacy and off-campus propaganda, combines to create a violent campus culture that has held sway for two generations.

Understanding the reality on Palestinian campuses requires recognizing the role these forces, principles, responsibilities, and allegiances play. In the end, intimidating or threatening the lives of those students and faculty who express unpopular political opinions remains by far the most serious threat to academic freedom on Palestinian campuses. It is Palestinians themselves who must bear responsibility for those actions.

10. ISLAMIC AND AL-AZHAR UNIVERSITIES OF GAZA

A long-running and sometimes violent struggle between Hamas and Fatah carries over with unfortunate frequency into Palestinian universities. An institution where the picture of internal struggle no longer applies, however, is Islamic University of Gaza (IUG) (Fig. 4), a university in Gaza City that was established in a hostile collaboration by the Muslim Brotherhood (MB) and nationalists in 1978, then firmly taken over by MB's successor Hamas in the early 1980s.[34] Tensions between Hamas and Fatah led some sixteen faculty members to resign (Sullivan 1994, 168). Azzam Tamimi, a London-based Hamas supporter, provides details:

> The first few years of the university were fraught with serious disputes, initially within the founding committee and then within the board of trustees. One of the major points of disagreement was

---

34. IUG's "founding board members were mainly members of the Ikhwan [Muslim Brotherhood] who were also involved with the al-Mujamma al-Islami (the Islamic Center) at the time presided over by Sheikh Yassin. The birth of the university was attended by some difficulties. The local Fatah organization, which was already beset by anxiety over the growing influence of the Ikhwan in Gaza, was prepared to go to any lengths to prevent the project from coming to fruition, unless Fatah was wholly able to control it. To avert the potential threat to their project, the Ikhwan asked the PLO Chairman and Fatah leader Yasser Arafat to endorse the founding document of the university and to issue a decree appointing a founding committee. He may not have been aware that at least half of the membership of the committee were leading Ikhwan figures from Palestine and Jordan, while the other half consisted of Fatah officials selected for their sympathy toward the Ikhwan" (Tamimi 39-40).

over who would fill the position of president of the university. The Ikhwan [Muslim Brotherhood] wanted one of their own number, while Arafat would not settle for anything less than one of his own supporters. At times, arguments spilled over on to the streets of Gaza in the form of violence between the partisans of Fatah and members of the Ikhwan. The Ikhwan leadership was determined to impose its full authority and to maintain total control of the university, even if its only recourse was to respond in kind to intimidation and violence. (40)

The intense hostility "led to the assassination of the Head of the Department of Arabic Language and Literature, Dr. Ismail Al Khatib . . . murdered by Fatah operatives who demanded representations within the university's executive committee" (Zelkovitz 100). According to Tamini,

> Muslim Brotherhood sources say that a hit list endorsed by the late Khalil al-Wazir (Abu Jihad), Fatah's second in command under Yasser Arafat, was sent to Gaza in the early 1980s . . . the hit list included the names of some Islamists working for or associated with Islamic University . . . . These included Dr. Isma'il al-Khatab . . . who was murdered in his own car in front of his house and in the presence of his nine children (326).

The antagonism never really abated. In May 1983 partisans on the IUG campus fought with iron bars and clubs and several people were hospitalized. The rise of Islamic fundamentalism added new actors and increased intensity to these conflicts. In early 1986, female nationalist demonstrators at IUG were attacked by neo-fundamentalists wielding clubs and chains (Sullivan *Under Occupation* 62). A series of clashes between the Islamic Bloc and nationalist women students was quelled when the women students and accompanying family members were dispersed with water hoses (Johnson A-129).

The conflicts between Hamas and Fatah culminated in the dismissal at IUG of "four staff members sympathetic to the nationalist movement. One of the four, faculty member Dr. Abu Sitte, noted that the dismissals were intended to make the university an 'exclusively fundamentalist institution'" (Johnson B-125). As Sullivan writes, at times "the Islamic University's leadership regarded its secular Palestinian opponents as perhaps as great a threat as the Israeli occupation authorities" (*Under Occupation* 61). Yet there were also divisions within fundamentalism. Not long after the Palestinian Islamic Jihad was founded, the Islamic Jihad movement was established at IUG in 1982 as a violent fundamentalist alternative to the Muslim Brothers and began organizing its own student cells.

Meanwhile, IUG evolved into an arsenal and a terrorist redoubt. During the 2007 open warfare between Fatah and Hamas, Fatah raided IUG and confiscated 2,000 AK-47 assault rifles, hundreds of RPG launchers, and massive amounts of ammunition (Shaked). CNN opened a February 2, 2007, story by reporting that "The current round of violence began with a fierce midnight shootout at Gaza's Islamic University and followed Thursday's clashes between Hamas and Fatah." For three days IUG and its neighbor and political opponent the Fatah-affiliated Al-Azhar University (AUG) became a battleground for Fatah and Hamas. At IUG, "Two rocket-propelled grenades were fired into the top floor of the library, setting a blaze that gutted the computer center" (Myre). "Fatah security forces stormed the Hamas aligned University in Gaza City on Friday, 2 February, setting ablaze and leaving in near total ruin the library, computer center, and other buildings" (Tamimi 257).[35] The bookstore, science labs, and a conference center were also burned. After Israeli Corporal Gilad Shalit was kidnapped in June 2006, he was held for months at IUG (Ynet News). Earlier, in 1995, the Hamas terrorist Yahya Ayyash took refuge there when he was being pursued for organizing suicide bombings. While there was considerable international outrage when Israel destroyed weapons labs at IUG in 2014, that operation caused notably less damage than the factional Palestinian fighting in 2007.

The value of a major university in Gaza dominated by a particular political faction was apparent immediately. Palestinian author and politician Ziad Abu-Amr has described IUG as "the principal Muslim Brotherhood stronghold" in Gaza (17). Once the Brotherhood had solidified its control of IUG, Fatah created its own institution, al-Azhar

---

35. Azzam Tamimi is chairman and editor in chief of Ahiwar TV Channel. Born in Hebron, Tamimi is a British Palestinian writer and activist who has been affiliated with the Muslim Brotherhood.

University of Gaza, in 1992, partly triggered by the sixteen faculty resignations from IUG.[36] The two institutions are located next to each other in Gaza City. Al-Azhar, which now serves over 18,000 students, was organized by Shaykh Muhammed Awad, earlier the chairperson on the Sharia Court of Appeals, at the explicit direction of Yasser Arafat. That left Gaza with what amounted to opposing political strongholds, constituting much more than a contrast between a religious (Islamic University) and a secular (al-Azhar University) institution, though the religious difference alone had notable consequences.

IUG is strictly gender segregated, with men and women studying in separate buildings, whereas men and women study together at al-Azhar, though both institutions observe the traditional dress code for women. At IUG, "Every lecture is given twice: once for men, a second time for women. Men and women enter the university through separate entrances, eat in separate cafeterias and use shared facilities like the library and science laboratories during separate hours . . . . Men are discouraged from speaking to women or looking them in the eye. There is no dating, dancing, or drinking. A call to prayer rings out across the campus five times a day" (Murphy). Hamas appoints board members at IUG, while Fatah appoints them at Al-Azhar.

As Israeli scholar Ido Zelkovitz writes, "Al-Azhar University endeavored to establish a traditional yet lively cultural sphere to counteract the Islamic fundamentalist atmosphere fostered by the Islamic University of Gaza." (126). Over time, rules were relaxed at Al-Azhar so that women could wear colorful headscarves rather than the black ones traditionally mandated by Islamic rules of modesty. This infuriated IUG students who rioted at an October 2008 AUG rally organized by Islamic Bloc Hamas students from IUG. As James Cemmell writes in a joint report for Britain's University and College Union and Education International, "a student group had stormed the university in violent protest and had raised the Hamas flag over the university's main building." A *New York Times* report adds important detail:

---

36. In addition to these two prominent institutions, higher education in Gaza is also served by several other post-secondary schools, including Palestine Technical College, University College of Applied Sciences, Al-Quds Open University, Gaza University, Isra University, and University of Palestine.

When members of the academic staff protested outside, Hamas
police beat them with clubs, said Ayman Shaheen, a professor of
political science. Mr. Shaheen said he was hit twice . . . . A number
of female students were then attacked at the rally by participants
who mostly came from outside, many armed with clubs, witnesses
said . . . . Riham Abu Arrus was struck in the leg with an ax,
according to friends who accompanied her to hospital. Ms. Abu
Arrus was first taken to Gaza's main Al Shifa hospital, which is now
under Hamas control, but was refused immediate treatment, the
friends said. (El-Khodary)

Tensions had already escalated during the 2006 Palestinian Legislative
Council election when both Gaza campuses were widely utilized for
campaigning. As Cemmell observes, "The conduct of extra-legal
political activity on campus during the 2006 elections forewarned
that post-election, universities would continue to represent sites where
political factions would continue their conflict." At the 2008 rally,
"The intimidation and violence used by the protestors provides for
clear restrictions on academics to work in an environment free from
discrimination and fear." Academic freedom, in short, was substantially
imperiled.

A month after the previous 2008 riot, another AUG battle broke
out between Hamas and Fatah students, this time suppressed by Hamas
police who beat students with clubs and gun butts. The violence was
triggered by an Islamic bloc student who fired a gun at another student, luckily missing him. It was part of a sequence of violent events.
In May, in a still earlier clash, a student hurled a grenade that exploded
in a group of students and injured thirteen, one seriously (PCHR). In
August a bomb had exploded on campus, just after a classroom emp-
tied. The 2008 riot was neither the only nor the last time Hamas police
accompanied by thugs in civilian dress would administer severe beatings at AUG, breaking bones with clubs. On March 16, 2011, they
assaulted Fatah-allied students on campus who were planning to walk
to a demonstration, with Hamas-allied students joining in the assault
(Eurasia).

The pattern that the two campuses are not only designated places
for academic pursuits but also places where political groups carry out

assaults on each other was established over a period of years. In March 2005 the Palestinian Centre for Human Rights issued a press release that begins "PCHR is deeply concerned at latest incidents that have taken place in al-Azhar University in Gaza City, which threatened the lives of both professors and students and have led to the closure of the university. PCHR also condemns attacks by a number of the university students on classrooms and threats directed at the president and his deputy." On October 12, 2005, Fatah gunmen angered by the expulsion of six Fatah-affiliated students involved in campus violence entered the office of AUG president Adnan al-Khadi and assaulted him until al-Khadi fled. This pattern continues to the present day. Moreover, the conflict between Fatah and Hamas has entrenched the practice of settling disagreements, including those over administration policies like tuition rates, by student demonstrations, which are repeatedly suppressed by the police. That was the case again in March 2018 when at least five students were wounded (Toameh "Hamas Police"). The following month divisions within Fatah itself produced violent assaults on supporters of dissident Fatah politician Mohammed Dahlan by supporters of PA president Mahmoud Abbas at yet another Gaza City institution, Al-Aqsa University, a government institution now serving 20,000 students (i24).[37]

Because both IUG and AUG reached their identities through politics and promoted hostile political and military groups, their reigning ideologies and practices combine politics, faith, and culture in ways that powerfully shape the lives of students, staff, and faculty. Moreover, as Loren Lybarger documents, the drive to "take over university student councils, labor unions, and professional associations" (81) helped consolidate and empower the Muslim Brotherhood and its successor Hamas. As Sara Roy adds, "Gaza's social norms have been imposed by various forms of coercion"; "it is by now axiomatic when speaking of Hamas social institutions to think of them as part of a larger political and military network engaged in terrorism" (77, 70).

Until 1977, most students from Gaza pursued higher education in Egypt, but at that point Egypt largely closed that option and thus

37. Al-Aqsa was founded as a teacher's institute under Egypt in 1955, becoming a college of education in 1991 and a university in 2001.

triggered the will to create higher education opportunities in Gaza itself. Co-founded by Sheikh Ahmed Yassin (1937–2004) (Fig. 4), the future founder of Hamas itself, the IUG enrolls over 20,000 students. It is recognized as Gaza's best institution of higher education, offering bachelor's and master's degrees in such fields as economics, education, engineering, history, literature, and physics. It has cooperative relationships with major institutions elsewhere, including the London School of Economics. Meanwhile, it has a mission to ensure, as Lybarger describes the aims of a Hamas leader at Bethlehem University on the West Bank, that "every aspect of existence—politics, economics, personal piety . . . be brought into conformity with the core principles of Islamic law" (90). Islam in Gaza is "the epitome of an overarching, integrating, and alternative rationality" (91). An IUG administrator told Michael Irving Jensen that "Scholarship means something different at this university. From the very first day it is practiced in the name of Allah" (105). At IUG, even the slogans promoted at demonstrations have often been religious in character (Johnson E-130).

In another critical sense, however, IUG falls into the category of a "dual-purpose institution." From the outset, it has served as a Hamas recruitment center. Many of Hamas's leaders either graduated from IUG or have been members of its faculty. IUG trains the Islamist mullahs who lead Gaza mosques, who in turn in circular fashion recruit Islamist students for IUG. Lt. Col. Jonathan Halevi, a former Israeli intelligence officer, in 2006 cited the example of a Hamas children's magazine *Al-Fateh*, which recently celebrated Islamic University as "the university of suicide attackers" (Murphy). The school has also held rallies at which students have sworn allegiance to "continue the jihad" against Israel (Murphy). As journalist Thanassis Cambanis wrote in the *Boston Globe* in 2010, Islamic University is

> the brain trust and engine room of Hamas, the Islamist movement that governs Gaza and has been a standard-bearer in the renaissance of radical Islamist militant politics across the Middle East. Thinkers here generate the big ideas that have driven Hamas to power; they have written treatises on Islamic governance, warfare, and justice that serve as the blueprints for the movement's political and militant platforms. And the university's goal is even more radical

and ambitious than that of Hamas itself, an organization devoted primarily to war against Israel and the pursuit of political power. Its mission is to Islamicize society at every level, with a focus on Gaza but aspirations to influence the entire Islamic world....

Hamas doesn't run the Islamic University, but the overlap of the party and the school is nearly seamless. Scientists and academics at the university double as Hamas technocrats: doctors, engineers, economists, teachers, and media specialists. The Islamic University serves as an employment program and intellectual retreat for Hamas leaders, giving a perch to the prime minister, the foreign minister, and bureaucrats in charge of ministries....

The scholarship and instruction at the Islamic University offer a map of the world Hamas's leaders would build if they had no political constraints. More than any single idea, the Islamic University promotes a view of a society inescapably suffused with religious doctrine.

IUG's status as a Hamas stronghold has also implicated it in acts of terrorism perpetrated by the regime. Indeed, a rocket development and testing facility on campus was bombed by the IDF twice during separate military campaigns. Hamas's military wing, the Izz ad-Din al-Qassam Brigades, was using the institution's chemistry labs and other facilities not only to develop but also to manufacture and supply weapons. Islamic University faculty may have been involved in its work. The weapons lab was among the Islamic University facilities struck during 2008–2009's Operation Cast Lead, unequivocally establishing its status as a military target (Katz). It was later rebuilt. Then, during Operation Protective Edge in 2014, Israel reported that rockets had actually been fired at Israel from the campus area and targeted it a second time.

Such a facility is a valid target according to the laws of war. Nonetheless, in 2014, the IDF chose to strike the facility at night, to minimize or eliminate the possibilities of casualties. Indeed, there were no reported injuries. Nevertheless, proponents of a boycott of Israeli universities in the American Historical Association (AHA) the following year made much of a claim that an oral history archive across the street had also been damaged or destroyed. "What good are we as historians," they argued, "if we do not protest the destruction of an archive?" It does not seem unreasonable to say that it seems unwise to leave an archive next to an established military target. Furthermore, the claim that this collateral damage, as opposed to the very existence of a weapons manufacturing facility on a university campus, was the salient element of the story is questionable at best. Meanwhile, the 2014 war provided an opportunity for Hamas to register its long-running hostility toward Al-Azhar. On August 22, 2014, Hamas executed over a score of suspected collaborators and dumped two of the bodies near AUG (Hoyle). It was a political warning.

Given its fundamental role in promoting the work of a terrorist organization, IUG belongs at the extreme end of politically compromised Palestinian institutions. There is such overwhelming political conformity at Islamic University that it is unreasonable to claim any meaningful academic freedom of political or religious expression exists there. But the case of Islamic University raises numerous difficult questions about the problems that arise when other Palestinian universities serve as incitement and recruitment centers. A 2013 essay by Aviv (Cohen) Dekel, then affiliated with Georgetown University Law Center, asks whether an educational grant to IUG would amount to financial support for terrorism under US or Israeli law. The answer may be "yes," without even raising the fact that Hamas routinely diverts humanitarian aid for military purposes.

11. ANTI-ZIONIST AND ISLAMIST CURRICULA

It is impossible to evaluate a university fully without well documented information about the character and caliber of its curriculum and degree programs.[38] Published reports suggest that Palestinian universities in Gaza and the West Bank offer credible job training in a number of practical and technical areas of study. In the previous generation, for example, "expansion of programs at Palestinian universities emphasized technical and vocational education such as banking, commerce, administration, infrastructure, and tourism" (Bruhn 1133). Education in engineering and in a range of health professions have been priorities for several decades.[39]

But preliminary evidence also raises serious concern about a different fundamental issue—the corruption of the curriculum, indeed of the educational mission as a whole, by anti-Zionist and Islamist politics. An-Najah marketing professor Sam Abd Al-Qadir Alfoqahaa mentions mandatory "courses on the Palestinian cause" as among those taught at multiple institutions (35)[40]; one may reasonably doubt that courses on the Palestinian cause taught on the West Bank and in Gaza

---

38. It would be useful to have detailed personal accounts by both local Palestinian and visiting faculty of the experience of teaching on the West Bank. I discuss one example at the end of this essay, but if others exist, I haven't found them.

39. See my *Israel Denial* for details about the steady improvement of Palestinian medical services and the collaborative educational efforts undertaken by Israelis and Palestinians.

40. Alfoqahaa is also director of public relations at An-Najah.

would encourage rigorous, dispassionate thinking. Without sufficient information to make a comprehensive report, we can nonetheless document blatant anti-Zionist and anti-Semitic indoctrination at two major institutions: the Islamic University of Gaza (IUG) and Birzeit University on the West Bank. While few would be wholly surprised that some curricula at Palestinian universities are fundamentally biased, these unsettling examples also undermine claims about the educational mission and the status of academic freedom at these highly politicized institutions. Antony Sullivan cites an IUG catalogue from the 1980s that offers History 4317, "A History of the Jews and the Zionist Movement," which says the course aims to "refute the propaganda of the racist [Zionist] movement which deceived the Jews themselves" (*Under Occupation* 59). As a colleague who reads Arabic confirmed, the current IUG catalogue is unfortunately password protected, but there is every reason to suppose Hamas inspired anti-Zionist attitudes there have not changed.

As Michael Irving Jensen of the Danish Institute for International Studies documents, IUG has in place an obligatory introductory series of courses called "*Islamicum*." The Islamicum curriculum takes a full year and turns the undergraduate degree into a five-year program. It is obligatory for all students except those who graduated from the Islamic secondary school, the Al-Azhar Religious Institute, that was the origin of IUG. Early on in Jensen's research, reported in essays and in his 2009 book *The Political Ideology of Hamas: A Grassroots Perspective*, he took the important but uncommon step of attending classes at IUG for six months and interviewing students and faculty there.

Islamicum, he makes clear, aims to present students with an Islamist worldview and to shape their identities around its values and perspectives. *Islamicum* also established the general curricular principle that "all subjects should be studied from an Islamic perspective" and communicates "a clear sense of the university's entire mission: namely, to revive Islamic civilization" (Jensen 110, 124) and to purify Islam of foreign and secular impulses by recovering its original purpose (Sullivan *Under Occupation* 56). As IUG declared, "The university's curriculum is planned to ensure that knowledge, development, culture and values are in accordance with Islam" (Jensen 103).

Islamicum is ideologically grounded in a clash of civilizations model, with the Islamic and Western worlds seen as locked in combat. While there are certainly conservative constituencies in Western countries that embrace a clash of civilizations worldview, though with a hostile perspective on Islamic culture, it is hard to find major universities comprehensively committed to instilling them in the student body. Moreover, Islam, as IUG understands and promotes it, is decidedly Islamist, devoted not merely to demonstrating that Islam is a superior culture but to the belief that Sharia law offers the only truly moral system of governance and ethical conduct.

IUG faculty and administrators like to promote the idea that IUG matches the ideological conformity of some contemporary religious institutions in the West, but the differences are profound—most significantly because IUG is integrated with the political and cultural enforcement power of Hamas. Religiously affiliated colleges in the US have the power to fire people for heresy but not to put their lives at risk. IUG implements Gaza's state religion. Comparisons with Western religious institutions of higher education would have to reach back to the time when church and state were inseparable, when Christianity had the power to punish heresy and classes were compelled to conform to its theology. At IUG, nothing falls outside the orbit of Islamist convictions.

Some of the curricular consequences are predictable and a welcome corrective to widely institutionalized pro-Western biases. The belief that Islamic civilization is "superior to all other civilizations" has the consequence, for example, that the scientific discoveries and advances of earlier Islamic cultures are given prominence and that Islamic achievements in the arts, from painting to architecture, are celebrated. But that barely even hints at how a thoroughgoing Islamist perspective on all knowledge actually works at IUG.

Jensen went on to audit two more advanced courses, "American Literature" and "Literary Appreciation," citing a representative lesson from each. The lectures he transcribed show that an Islamist view of culture does not just involve promoting achievements ignored or diminished in the West but also involves teaching students inappropriate and even bizarre interpretive skills and strategies.

His account of the instructor's guided class discussion of Nathaniel Hawthorne's *The Scarlet Letter* (1850) is particularly striking because the lesson extracted from the novel is a surprising one, though in retrospect it is predictable if you seriously consider what an Islamist perspective might bring to the book. Students were asked what punishment the protagonist Hester Prynne should have received for committing adultery. In the novel she is compelled to wear a scarlet letter "A" as a permanent marker of her shame. The students equivocated, so the professor clarified the question by requesting an Islamic response and offered the answer: she should be stoned to death: "In the novel she will live with the shame forever. In our Islam there is a rule that such a woman should be stoned. This is the punishment within the Islamic frame of reference. Death is better for her. She prefers to die rather than carry the scarlet letter" (116). As Jensen writes, "The Islamic response . . . is highlighted as superior and more humane compared with the Puritans' way of settling Hester's fate" (117).

As one might expect, anti-Zionist and anti-Semitic lessons are the other constant component of IUG's clash of civilizations message. Here, the contortions necessary to read texts through an anti-Semitic lens are frankly unimaginable. Jensen gives a detailed account of the discussion of British poet Roger McGough's poem "The Cats' Protection League" (CPL), the opening poem from his twelfth collection of children's poetry, the award-winning *Bad Bad Cats* (1997). McGough, it should be noted, is not primarily a children's poet, though he has written poetry for children throughout his career. Here is his entertaining "The Cats' Protection League" (CPL) in its entirety, also quoted in full in Jensen's book:

Midnight, a knock at the door
Open it? Better had
Three heavy cats, mean and bad
They offer protection. I ask "what for?"
The boss cat snarls, "You know the score"
Listen man and listen good
If you wanna stay in this neighbourhood
Pay your dues or the toms will call
And wail each night on the backyard wall

Mangle the flowers, and as for the lawn
A smelly minefield awaits you at dawn
These guys meant business without doubt
Three cans of tuna, I handed them out
Then they disappeared like bats in hell
Those bad, bad cats from CPL.[41]

Class discussion begins by noting that the language is colloquial, though no one notices that the poem is meant to be funny. One wonders if anyone registers the way the end rhymes punctuate the humor. Did they even understand the meaning of "A smelly minefield awaits you at dawn" (no litter box intended)? Instead, the comments quickly become irrelevant and inappropriate. The conversation takes close reading on a journey through the looking glass. While Jensen's account aims for neutral, non-judgmental reporting, I find more pointed comments necessary. Whether the class is more outrageous or sad I cannot decide. The discussion's field of reference segues quickly from American street gangs to "Jewish gangs" to Israel to an Islamist take on US foreign policy. But there is no textual warrant for these interpretive moves. We have left behind anything that could qualify as responsible pedagogy.

---

41. From Roger McGough, *Bad Bad Cats*, p. 3. "The Cats' Protection League," reprinted in full in Jensen's book, is also the title of McGough's book's first section, comprising six poems. For comparison, consider his "Mafia Cats" (pp. 6-7), whose second stanza reads

We run all the rackets
From gambling to vice
On St. Valentine's Day
We massacre mice

"Fur Exchange" (4-5) opens with "Kitten gone missing?" then devotes several stanzas to ways cats meet their end, including

Twenty-ton truck
Charging down the street
Maybe the kitten
Got under its feet?

But it turns out the CPL has the kitten, adapting its protection racket:

We charge a fiver
For returning kittens
Or else it's a pair
Of tortoiseshell mittens.

We are witnessing what is effectively a hate group in a culture that fuses anti-Semitism and anti-imperialism.

> Professor: "Yes, it's dialect. Everyday language, even though it's not in a friendly tone. It reminds us of American gangs."
> Student: "Jewish gangs."
> Prof: "Yes, just like during the Intifada."
> Student: "Jewish as usual."
> Student: "It reminds me of Fagin in *Oliver Twist*." (113)

The students clearly know what their teacher wants from them. Indeed, they are likely veterans of the first year curriculum. But they are nonetheless struggling because Islam regards cats, unlike dogs, positively. They continue, with an eighth student adding: "I think it refers to the current situation in the Middle East. The West and the United States versus the Arabs. The cats are the West, and the man is a symbol of the Arabs."

> Prof: "That's a good point. Just like during the Iraq crisis."
> Student: "I take a similar view. The cats symbolize the Jewish lobby in the States, and the man is an image of the United States."
> Prof: "But we need to look at this as Muslims." (114)

Matters continue in this vein, as efforts are made to twist the poem into a critique of Western capitalism, but the anti-Semitic conclusions continue:

> Student: "I think the cats symbolize Jews, whereas the man is a symbol of the Muslims and particularly the refugees."

It would be possible to discover that McGough (1937–), the poet, has condemned both fascism and anti-Semitism, but then neither the instructor nor the students have any notion that knowing something about a writer's views and publications might constrain what it is reasonable to say about a work of literature. In fact, there is no evidence anywhere in McGough's work that he has ever written poems about Israel or the Middle East conflict at all.[42] But the instructor (Mr. Muhammad) is

---

42. I have no way of knowing whether the instructor provided the poem from a copy of *Bad Bad Cats* or another source. Since the class took place several years before Hamas took over Gaza, the instructor would have had some access to Israeli resources for background research if Gaza libraries proved too limited. In addition to his books of children's poetry, McGough had published a dozen

apparently uninterested: "At no point in the lesson did Mr. Muhammad explain when the poem was written, or who had composed it" (179). At IUG, "The Cats' Protection League" was not a poem written by anyone in particular. It was just an anonymous text, unmoored to anything except the anti-Zionist goals of the class. Unsurprisingly, then, no one points out that it is problematic to find contemporary references in a poem written more than a decade earlier. Like the *Scarlet Letter* reading, all these contorted analogies have nothing whatsoever to do with the poem, the entertaining book *Bad Bad Cats*, or McGough's career. McGough is among several poets early on identified with Liverpool culture of the 1960s; he wrote much of the dialogue for the Beatles' animated film *Yellow Submarine*. If "The Cats' Protection League" can be read as an anti-Semitic text, then absolutely anything could be. Notably, neither the professor nor the class are at pains to distinguish between anti-Zionism and anti-Semitism or between Israelis and other Jews. All Jews are hostile, criminal, or worse. The discussion focuses on demonizing the West and its purportedly premier villains the Jews. It is not an exercise in interpretation; it is about misreading in order to instill hate. The class pedagogy certainly fulfills IUG's Islamist imperative, but it does more, unreflectively mirroring the anti-Semitic bias of the surrounding Gazan culture.

John Murphy recounts a similarly structured IUG class led by Professor Akram Habeeb in 2006, the class discussion punctuated by Israeli artillery shells exploding in response to rockets from Gaza that injured family members in an Israeli mobile home. Habeeb was lecturing on early American literature: "Habeeb commented that the early settlers wrote about the Native Americans as barbaric and uncivilized. Still, many wrote glowingly of their new life and the riches of the land, encouraging other Europeans to follow them. 'Does it remind you of anybody?' he asked. 'The Jews' one woman answered. 'Yes, when they talk about the land of milk and honey.'"

There are texts one could responsibly use as analogies for or guides to the contemporary scene if you accept that kind of pedagogical

---

volumes of poetry for adults by then. His 2003 Collected Poems did not appear until later. Its representation of his children's poetry, however, is very limited. *Bad Bad Cats*, for example, is represented by only one poem.

practice. Indeed, Sari Nusseibeh gives examples from his teaching at Birzeit. Here is one:

> Another classroom favorite was *The Wretched of the Earth*, an essay on the Algerian war by psychologist Frantz Fanon. Once again, the students saw themselves in the role of the Algerians fighting off the French army and the settler population it had been sent to protect . . . . The people of Algeria . . . heroically fought off the settlers, and gained their independence. The message for my students was obvious. (179)

But to treat one of Roger McGough's children's poems as a deliberate lesson about Jewish criminality is obscene.

Higher education at IUG is apparently consumed with anti-Semitic paranoia and conspiracy theories. Thus the IUG curriculum needs to be broadly investigated and, if this pattern proves widespread, condemned, and IUG financially isolated from the international higher education community. Unfortunately, pressuring an institution under Hamas control to reform itself is not a realistic option. IUG does not merit unqualified idealization as an institution. It is important to distinguish, however, between promoting international exchanges to foster interaction between faculty and students and funding an institution's programs. A good deal of the promotional material by IUG faculty and administrators conveniently omits problematic information. IUG's Professor Sanaa Abou-dagga, for example, writes a detailed report on IUG without ever mentioning the Islamist curriculum. Does the *Islamicum* curriculum merit a grant from the European Union or any foreign university? Naively providing IUG with monetary grants is ill advised, but the freedom to pursue international personal contacts should be sustained.

If Jensen of the Danish Institute for International Studies aims for neutrality, Duke University's Rebecca Stein in "How One Palestinian University is Remaking 'Israel Studies'" offers instead an enthusiastic, entirely uncritical endorsement of an anti-Zionist program at Birzeit University. As Stein had already been pursuing an anti-Zionist agenda within Duke's own Jewish studies program, her endorsement of Birzeit's program without qualification appears to be a matter of political solidarity, rather than a traditional academic evaluation. Birzeit's

Israel Studies website provides a two-sentence mission statement that opens with reasonable academic language, then shifts quickly to anti-Zionist polemic:

> Our mission is to provide Palestinian and Arab academic knowledge production with researchers capable of contributing original, critical knowledge about the various aspects of Israeli society. At the core of our educational philosophy is to strengthen critical awareness of power, hegemony, and the moral-political aspects of knowledge production in confronting occupation, settler colonialism, and violence.

Israel is prejudged in the program's self-definition. It is bad enough when a single course enforces anti-Zionist political opinion—as my *Israel Denial: Anti-Zionism, Anti-Semitism, and the Faculty Campaign Against the Jewish State* documents for a number of US courses—but the assault on free inquiry is still more serious when the entirety of a purportedly academic program does so. Education, a recent Birzeit program graduate tells Stein shamelessly, is "part of knowing your enemy, part of the knowledge of resistance." Fakher Eldin, a Birzeit faculty member, is more specific: "My basic strategy is to show them that all of the atrocities of Zionism and the occupation are basically comparable atrocities." Stein blandly adds that "a settler-colonial framework is central within the curriculum" and crows that "the very notion of 'Israel Studies' is being wholly remade."

The only thing that may actually be new about the Birzeit curriculum, however, is not its anti-Zionism but rather the oppressive uniformity and conformity of its mission. There are plenty of faculty in Israel Studies and Jewish Studies programs in the US opposed not just to Israeli policies but to the existence of the Jewish state; they teach from that perspective, but students can usually find some other faculty member to supervise either a neutral or a Zionist-oriented project. At Birzeit that would be a tall order. Social pressure to conform to an unqualified anti-Zionism that crosses the line into anti-Semitism is relentless.

The Israel Studies program at Birzeit gains some legitimacy from what appears to be the more conventional politicization of other humanities and social science programs there. Thus its Institute of Women's

Studies, founded as a program in 1994 and elevated to Institute status in 1998, concludes its website "Who We Are" statement by confirming that "the Institute continues to play an active role as part of initiatives within Palestinian civil society, in struggles for gender and social equity, as well as national rights." Its director, Eileen Kuttab, celebrates this mix of research and activism but manages to avoid portraying the program as politically monolithic, while elsewhere including "resisting the occupation" as part of its mission. Penny Johnson is more forthcoming in a series of essays as she sorts through "the dual role of universities in activism and learning" in the context of Birzeit during the 1980s, since she acknowledges that there are fundamental tensions between the two roles. In a moment that should not escape notice, Kuttab echoes the Jimmy Carter position noted earlier by telling us "the promotion of political tolerance and respect for different views" at Birzeit is certified by the repeated democratic elections giving control of the student government to Hamas. Given the level of violence and coercion that has accompanied the campus struggles between Fatah and Hamas, Kuttab's testimony is at best disingenuous, at worst less than honest. An observer could reasonably ask whether Birzeit's official institutional embrace of anti-normalization with Israel allows for a truly open airing of diverse views.

There is one area in which some at Birzeit have second thoughts: they argue whether using the name "Israel Studies" for a program in itself lends the "Zionist entity" an unwelcome aura of normalization, thus contradicting Birzeit's strong institutional policy of anti-normalization. Some preferred the alternative program title of "settler-colonial studies." The program offers a spectrum of courses, from "Zionist Ideology and History" to "Jewish History and Thought," though one may reasonably assume that neither course represents anything that would pass international standards for objectivity. Stein's article, which first appeared on the Middle East Research and Information Project website in May 2019, was immediately reprinted and effectively adopted by Birzeit itself.

A widespread trend in the West has been to treat Palestinian universities—including An-Najah, Birzeit, and Islamic University of Gaza—as institutions comparable to our own, beleaguered but still noble in intent, dedicated to an educational mission we can identify with and support. As the evidence here suggests, that is not the case. IUG is not simply politicized; it is militarized; its mission is indoctrination. An-Najah and Birzeit, on the other hand, are deeply fraught and compromised, politicized so thoroughly as to make their difference from Western standards one of character and kind, not degree. All three institutions are among those Palestinian universities that create socially, politically, and conceptually coercive environments in which academic freedom as we know it cannot thrive. The coercion is amplified by the atmosphere of physical threat and intimidation documented here.

All three universities are also recruitment enterprises. Universities worldwide certainly serve recruitment purposes as well, drawing students to the professions, to government service, and, in the case of ROTC programs in the US, to careers in the military. But few institutions elsewhere can claim peer recruitment to paramilitary groups or terrorist cells.

Education at An-Najah, Birzeit, and IUG, whether secular or religious, is part of "the inner jihad to transform hearts and minds" (Lybarger 104). Does anyone suppose that an IUG student could persistently oppose the idea that Sharia law is superior to Western legal systems? If a student there complained that stoning a woman to death is barbaric, not kindly, would that opinion be treated respectfully? Could a student there point out that it is illegitimate to weaponize a children's poem to give it an anti-Semitic mission when the poem has nothing to do with Jews? Could a student in Birzeit's MA program in Israel Studies get approval for a thesis arguing against the BDS/Birzeit anti-normalization campaign? Does Birzeit's program aim to produce scholars, as it claims, or propagandists who do not understand the need to question political assumptions and conclusions? What standards of evidence do Palestinian faculty encourage students to observe? What cultural roles do these institutions serve? What impact do they have on their societies? As Palestinian scholar Samir Anabtawi wrote decades ago, identifying a principle that remains as true now as it was then, "a university can only do well what society wishes it to do if it is in a position to question the norms, indeed the very assumptions and beliefs on which society itself rests" (74–75).

Part of the problem is that Palestinian universities still carry the legacy of their saturation with anti-Zionist activism during the First and Second Intifadas. It was inevitable that scheduling courses in homes and mosques during campus closures would result in class sessions devoted to the conflict with Israel. Students and faculty after all were living the conflict every day. Though the days of long closures are now over and unlikely to return short of a catastrophic third Intifada, which the Palestinian Authority itself will hopefully continue to resist, the occupation is ongoing, and the heroism of violent resistance continues to be celebrated on campus.

12. STUDENTS TRAVELING FROM GAZA[43]

Although Islamic University, for example, offers a range of different academic programs, there are also areas of study and advanced degrees not represented in its curriculum. As the Tel Aviv-based Israeli advocacy and research organization GISHA reports, across the 26 academic institutions in Gaza, some programs—including advanced degrees in clinical psychology, human rights, public health, gender studies, and international development—are not offered at all. For that and other reasons, including a student's right to apply to study at the institution of his or her choice, Palestinian students commonly apply to study at institutions in Arab countries, Europe, and the West, with some earning fellowships to support their study.

Some groups, GISHA among them, believe the right to study at any institution where you gain admission and meet financial requirements, including universities in the West Bank, rises to the level of a fundamental human right. Unsurprisingly, denunciations of Israeli restrictions on student travel from Gaza have been a regular feature of academic boycott resolutions, though such resolutions typically ignore the significant impediments other countries impose on travel from

---

43. According to a legal document translated by the Israeli NGO GISHA in September 2019, a number of positive changes have been implemented to facilitate faculty travel from Gaza. Thus they can apply for a permit to attend seminars or conferences abroad, and the criterion for academic studies has been broadened to include certification courses for engineers and technicians. Spouses and children can join recipients of scholarships for academic study. See GISHA, "Status for Authorizations" for full details.

Gaza. I have been in conversation with GISHA for some years and have high respect for their work, but I have a different take on the role that human rights play in the matter.

During the years when Israel occupied Gaza, travel in and out of the area for students and others was relatively routine. Many Israelis still remember when they made it a practice to shop in Palestinian markets there every week, and when many Gazans worked in Israel. All that began to change when Israel withdrew from Gaza in 2005. After Hamas won local elections the following year and took full control of Gaza in a 2007 civil war with Fatah, travel became both a political and a security issue. From the perspective of both Israel and the Palestinian Authority, Palestinians traveling from Gaza present security concerns. From the PA's perspective, Hamas is a violent and hostile political rival that presents a clear and present danger to all West Bank residents. For the Israelis, Hamas is a terrorist organization dedicated to killing Israelis and bringing an end to the Jewish state. Many countries worldwide have joined in designating Hamas a terrorist organization.

While both Israel and the PA recognize that students have a genuine right to study where they can gain admission and meet financial and other requirements, they also realize that young people exposed to Hamas propaganda can be motivated to engage in promoting, recruiting for, and participating in Hamas's violent agenda. West Bank Palestinian security forces already face a huge task trying to curtail violence; they are anxious about the risks involved in admitting Hamas-indoctrinated students for study in the West Bank. As this paper has documented, Hamas organizes terror cells in the West Bank that are devoted to bombing and killing. As with the issue of political expression in West Bank universities, academic freedom and security concerns intersect and conflict. BDS advocates tend to ignore or reject such dangers, but both Israel and the PA have a responsibility to confront them, a situation which inevitably limits students' rights to study where they choose.

Other major players besides Israel are similarly involved in adjudicating and administering student travel from Gaza. Since 2005, the standard travel route for Gaza students to study abroad has been to cross into Egypt at Rafah on Gaza's southern border and then fly elsewhere from Cairo Airport. But Egypt has kept the Rafah crossing largely closed from 2007–2019, and it was largely closed again in response to the coronavirus pandemic. Egypt too has had problems with Hamas and the Muslim Brotherhood. Hamas grew out of the Brotherhood, and the two groups remained allies. Egypt is justifiably opposed to Hamas collaboration with the violent Islamist insurgency in the Sinai and has ample reason to be vigilant about security at Cairo Airport (Joshua Robbin Marks). At a notorious 2014 Modern Language Association debate in which I participated, the faculty members proposing a boycott of Israeli universities were not only oblivious to the role that Egypt and others continue to play in restricting Palestinian student travel; they were also reluctant to concede that Egypt, not Israel, occupies Gaza's southern border.[44] Egypt itself could have largely solved the problem of student travel from Gaza, making Israel irrelevant, but it chose not to do so—at least until February 2019, when it reopened the Rafah crossing.[45] Should the decision to keep the crossing open permanently hold, once increased restrictions during the worldwide coronavirus pandemic come to an end—and if Egypt increases the number allowed passage—the problems with Gazan student travel through Egypt to other countries will have been substantially reduced.

One other problem with Rafa remains, however. Egypt charges a significant fee for passage. Gazans consequently often prefer to transit through Israel's Erez crossing, which they can do for free, even though that means flying from Amman, Jordan, rather than Cairo. As Israeli government officials confirmed in interviews, of 3,000 late 2019 Gazan requests to transit through Erez, only fourteen were denied, all for security reasons.

This is but one example of the fraught complexity of travel in the area. Hamas itself also obstructs student travel from Gaza. In order

---

44. For further detail about the 2014 MLA meeting, see Nelson and Brahm, eds. *The Case Against Academic Boycotts of Israel.*

45. Since May 2018, tens of thousands of Gazans have used the border to travel internationally; experts estimate 35,000 to 40,000 Gazans have left since mid-2018. Those who leave are mostly young Palestinian men in their 20s, especially those who have faced beatings and imprisonment from Hamas for their political leanings. As a result, many claim asylum if they reach European countries (Estrin and Bashir).

for students to travel through Israel and the West Bank and cross the Allenby Bridge to fly abroad from Amman, Jordan, Hamas must produce lists of students approved for admission to foreign universities. As a 2013 US State Department Bureau of Democracy, Human Rights, and Labor report detailed, Hamas has been very slow in doing so. Israel has increased the number of students it allows to exit Gaza from the north through the Erez crossing it controls.[46] But these students also need Jordanian transit permits to complete their travel, and Jordan is also slow to grant them. As Jack Khoury reported in *Haaretz* in May, 2016, "for months now, Jordan has been very stingy with these visas, known in Arabic as 'non-impediment' permits." Jordan's history of lethal conflict with Palestinians likely plays a role here. Meanwhile, the PA's Palestinian Civil Affairs Committee itself provides Israel with lists of students who have received fellowship support for study abroad, and they too are frequently late in doing so. The combined result of bureaucratic delays from Hamas, the PA, and Jordan frequently means that the school year is well under way or that fellowships expire before students from Gaza can reach their destinations. The BDS movement chooses to blame Israel alone for these difficulties.

As David Robinson details in a 2010 report from the sixth Education International and the Canadian Association of University Teachers, the continuing conflict between Hamas and Fatah has undermined university governance, produced the arrests of Palestinian faculty and students, and infringed on academic freedom in Gaza and the West Bank. As MSNBC reporter Kari Huus informs us, Hamas has a history of blocking students from accepting fellowships or traveling to participate in reconciliation programs, thereby instituting a politically-based restriction on student travel, a specific violation of academic freedom. The State Department's 2013 report also notes that Hamas

> prevented high school students from the Gaza Strip from participating in certain cultural and educational exchange

---

46. In 2018, after a period of calm, the Erez Crossing went from just permitting humanitarian cases to many other pedestrians crossing through. An average of 1000 people cross a day, according to COGAT. Over 2500 people crossed on December 8, 2019. Statistics are posted daily on COGAT's website. Over 30,000 cross every month. A visa is required.

programs, including programs sponsored by foreign governments and international organizations. Students on foreign exchange programs continued to face difficulty when traveling out of Gaza to obtain permission for onward travel abroad. In some instances families of the students petitioned Hamas's Ministry of Education so that their children could travel.

While Israel limits travel from Gaza to the West Bank through its territory for valid security reasons, and Israel's Supreme Court accepts the State's position that Israel has no obligation to guarantee Gazans the right to study in the West Bank, it should nonetheless be possible to mitigate the situation by instituting at least a pilot program for renewed study on the West Bank. Israel has recently once again allowed Gazans to take jobs in Israel, suggesting that carefully designed and monitored student entry programs are feasible if security conditions are met. GISHA's position, which I clarified during a visit to their offices, is that prohibitions on study in the West Bank should be applied individually, rather than comprehensively; that would clearly be the best practice to follow.

That does not, however, mean that I am urging what Birzeit University in *Making Education Illegal* (1995), more than a decade before Hamas took over Gaza, advocated for Gaza students denied travel permits. *Making Education Illegal* notably was published several years after Hamas was founded (1987) and two years after suicide bombings began. Birzeit insisted on a standard of proof that an "individual is likely to commit acts of violence toward Israeli citizens," which is too high a bar to guarantee public safety, and demanded "giving the individual his or her full legal rights including information about the charges being leveled against him or her and full recourse to challenge any action or decision in open court without the presence of secret 'security' information" (25).

The use of information from confidential informants and various surveillance techniques in open court, along with evidence of Hamas training, made that standard ill-advised. Closed hearings can be requested if sensitive sources and methods information is at stake. Notably, Birzeit in *Making Education Illegal* regards all acts of violence as individual (6-7), not group planned, even implying the same for suicide bombings (8). Birzeit insisted that "To link access to education to

the holding of a particular political viewpoint is contrary to the sections
of the *Universal Declaration of Human Rights* dealing with education"
(8). But endorsement of the Hamas charter with its commitment to kill
Jews is not simply a political viewpoint, despite US literary critic Judith
Butler's view to the contrary.

Before 2000, when the Second Intifada broke out, after which
Israel blocked students from Gaza from studying on the West Bank,
one thousand Gazan students a year studied there. Israel justifiably sets
criteria for study, but its security services are accomplished in doing
background checks and interviewing people before clearing them for
transit. As GISHA explained to me during a 2016 visit to their offices,
such interviews often inquire not only into personal histories but also
into the character of the neighborhoods in which people live. Continued
monitoring of Palestinian students from Gaza, especially as part of a
trial expanded program for study in the West Bank, would be expected.

On the other hand, one sometimes encounters academics naïve
enough to urge that Israel open Ben Gurion Airport for travel to and
from Gaza, something Israel allows only for exceptional humanitarian purposes. Making Hamas use of the airport routine would be
exceedingly dangerous and ill-advised. When political naïveté meets an
uninformed passion for justice, the results in terms of faculty political
activism are neither inspiring nor helpful. The end goal should not be
contempt for the security needs of Egypt, Israel, Jordan, and the PA—
let alone the pretense that Israel alone is responsible for the difficulties
that Palestinian students face—but rather a practical effort to balance
academic freedom and security in such a way that both interests are
served to the degree that is possible.

13. FOREIGN FACULTY TRAVEL TO ISRAEL AND THE WEST BANK

The challenge of negotiating the relationship between academic freedom and security has also sometimes been relevant to the cases of foreign faculty who wish to lecture in Israel or on the West Bank or teach at Palestinian universities. Indeed, complaints from Palestinian universities and from BDS activists about the resultant Israeli restrictions on faculty travel have recently been among the most widely publicized purported Israeli offenses against Palestinian academic freedom. An account of academic freedom at Palestinian universities would be incomplete without addressing these claims and trying to shed some light on the reality of the issues and practices at stake.

Israel has on occasion faced the challenge of deciding whether foreign faculty members who support Hamas, other terrorist groups, armed resistance, or the general romance of "revolutionary violence" should be allowed to speak or teach at Palestinian campuses if there is reason to believe they may engage in incitement to violence. As with student travel from Gaza to the West Bank, the twin issues of academic freedom and security define the problem. On September 12, 2016, Israeli officials barred University of London School of Oriental and African Studies faculty member Adam Hanieh, a strong supporter of Hamas and a member of the Al-Awda Right of Return Coalition, from speaking at Birzeit University and expelled him from the country. Scholars at Risk rather casually—and I believe irresponsibly and misleadingly—describes Hanieh as having simply "publicly criticized Israel

in the past" (Free to Think 2017), but that was hardly the defining problem. By then, Hanieh had been celebrating Hamas for at least a decade,
beginning with praise for the group's election victory (Hanieh).[47] In the
US, preventing Hanieh from speaking would constitute an improper
exercise of prior restraint; in the West Bank, the realistic risk of incitement in an environment where Hamas is an organized terrorist group
and violence both on and off campus is common once again creates a
different dynamic. While people are free to criticize such state actions,
it is clearly Israel's responsibility to negotiate such conflicts between
national security and academic freedom.

In the US, hate speech is protected, but state responsibility to monitor and mitigate its impact significantly increases when there is evidence
its pattern of inciting lethal violence has become tangible, most notably
when there are organized groups who pursue that end. Other countries
have sometimes faced comparable responsibilities, as Britain did at the
height of IRA violence. The existence of even unorganized constituencies prone to violence and susceptible to incitement requires increased
monitoring of internet traffic and social media and readiness to inter-
vene to prevent lethal assaults. Such threats to public safety have long
been magnified in Israel and in the Palestinian territories, but they have
now migrated to Europe and the US as well.

Some Western critics appeal exclusively to decontextualized abstract
principles to gin up opposition to Israeli efforts to navigate such complex
matters. Thus some claim that Israel violates academic freedom when
it prohibits a faculty member from entering the country. But academic
freedom does not guarantee a faculty member's right to enter a foreign country to take up an invitation to teach at one of its universities.
Academic freedom does not override a government's responsibility to
review security concerns and grant or refuse visas. All visa applications
in Israel are considered on a case-by-case basis, and reasons for turning
an application down are often technical. If, for example, a foreigner who
applied for a visa tries to enter the country before the visa is approved,
something that has happened in the past, he or she will be denied entry;

---

47. Hanieh has published eighteen articles about Middle East issues in the
Socialist Project's online journal *The Bullet*. For links to all of them see https://
socialistproject.ca/author/adam-hanieh/page/2/.

the odds are that the border official will not know the reason for denial. It may then be necessary to submit a new application. We can contest a government's reasoning, and there may be good reason to do so if we learn the nature of the reasoning, as we sometimes do when the US has denied faculty visas, but academic freedom does not trigger an automatic right of entry across international borders. There is cause to protest government reasoning without indulging in a category error.

In cases for which security concerns played a role, it is not, for example, adequate to claim that, since there are already Hamas student groups and Hamas-sympathetic local faculty at Palestinian universities, the addition of foreign faculty ready to promote Hamas violence makes no difference. Some visiting faculty carry notable prestige and all add international credibility and a sense of international consensus to the case for violence when they advocate for it. There is a double reinforcement at work. Anti-Zionist terrorists already see themselves as part of a global network, one enhanced by "its own online language and subculture" (Community Security Trust 4). International faculty endorsement adds academic prestige to the local and international ideological messaging. Yet so long as the reasons for specific visa denials remain secret, some will conclude the denials are political. People will assume Israel's anti-BDS law is always the justification even if it is not.

In addition to having a history of endorsing and promoting Hamas or other terrorist groups, a verifiable record of private fundraising for such groups would also justify excluding a foreign faculty member from teaching on the West Bank. Similarly, lying on a visa application or to border inspectors during an entry interview—or omitting critical information on either occasion, as Palestinian Jordanian Rasmea Odeh did when entering the US—would also justify denying entry or reentry.[48] Israeli law bars the entry of faculty from Iran and Syria, as those are classified as enemy countries. People from countries with no formal relations with

---

48. Odeh was convicted for her role in murdering two students in two 1969 Jerusalem bombings. She concealed that information when she applied to enter the United States, a crime for which she was convicted in 2014. In the years since her US conviction in federal court, still more evidence has surfaced proving her involvement in the murders. See Steven Lubet's forthcoming book *The Trials of Rasmea Odeh: How a Convicted Palestinian Commando Gained and Lost U.S. Citizenship.*

Israel, including those Arab countries in that category, have to obtain a prior permit (as government records shared with me confirmed, about 95% of those applications are approved). Other issues, like a documented history of repeated travel to Iran, would warrant investigation.

Whether the Israeli government is capable of consistently deciding all such individual cases reasonably and fairly remains to be seen. Certainly border authorities in other countries make bad decisions. The misguided law empowering immigration officials to bar BDS supporters from entering the country presents a serious challenge to that capacity. Guidelines issued by the Ministry of Strategic Affairs, drafted by an interagency group, narrow application of the law to leaders of organizations whose "support and promotion of boycotts" are carried out "in an active, continuous, and ongoing manner." Special attention is given to "activists who come to Israel on behalf of one of the prominent delegitimization organizations." Although garden variety BDS petition signers or movement followers are thus not to be denied entry, ongoing events justify concern about how the law is being interpreted and actually being put into practice. Certainly there are Israeli politicians who would like to see it more broadly enforced. The government's 2018 decision to prevent American student Lara Alqasem from entering Israel to pursue studies at Hebrew University of Jerusalem was, happily, overturned by the Israeli Supreme Court, but that only provided limited assurance about how the law could be applied, though it did establish a positive precedent. However, as government officials confirmed in interviews and emails, between March 14, 2017 (when the anti-BDS law went into effect) and August 2020, the Ministry for Strategic Affairs identified only sixteen people to be denied entry into Israel on BDS-related grounds. Of those, only one, Katherine Franke of Columbia University, a member of the steering committee of Jewish Voice for Peace's Academic Advisory Board, was a faculty member, and the Ministry reversed its decision and approved her entry in August 2020. The Franke case was widely denounced as one of the new millennium's signal violations of academic freedom and an obvious sign of the end of free speech in Israel, but it was neither of those things. Israel continually admits its critics to the country. Franke was denied entry as a leader of an exceptionally hostile organization that is self-described as "anti-Zionist," indeed specifically seeking the dissolution of the Jewish state. It has yet to happen that an academic who merely signed a BDS petition has been denied entry.

As both Brigadier General Sima Vaknin-Gil, former Director General of Israel's Ministry of Strategic Affairs (MSA) and an Israeli university president I consulted independently confirmed, there was clear awareness that the anti-BDS law could create conflicts with academic freedom. The MSA consequently met several times with Vera, the Association of Israeli University Presidents, to work out consultations and vetting procedures. An Israeli university inviting a foreign faculty member to an academic event can request and receive a pre-ruling to assure smooth entry to the country. The MSA agreed that academic freedom would be the basis for admitting invited faculty participating in Israeli events even if the "actively, continuously, and consistently" promoting BDS criteria were all met.

A visa granting temporary residency on the West Bank, however, involves different procedures and security concerns. The relevant criteria for visas are set by the Interior Ministry for entry into Israel; COGAT (Coordination of Government Activities in the Territories) does additional vetting of applicants who wish to enter the West Bank. As a government official confirmed in a January 2020 telephone interview, all foreigners enter the West Bank on a tourist visa. The standard tourist visa duration for both Israel itself and the West Bank is three months. Students and faculty can and should apply to the Palestinian Authority for an extended visa. A faculty member intending to teach can declare that fact on his or her visa application; the default, with COGAT approval, for teaching faculty is to grant a visa for one school year. The plan to teach at a college or university will then be noted on the extended tourist visa. The visa can also be renewed. In recent years, however, Israel has also sought to more consistently enforce its limit of five years duration for temporary residency for all foreign citizens, including visiting faculty teaching either in Israel proper or in the West Bank. Israel, like other countries, does not want to grant what amounts to permanent residency by default by indefinitely renewing tourist or work visas. That has recently produced an increased number of problems for some foreigners teaching long-term on the West Bank, though the Legal Center for Arab Minority Rights in Israel (Adalah) in 2019 filed a case before the Israeli High Court challenging whether this regulation can legally be applied to the West Bank. In the meantime, with the case still pending, COGAT has approved applications beyond the five years if they are otherwise in order. The Interior Ministry may choose to reject a visa application from a faculty member playing a leadership role in a BDS organization.

Despite some effort in this regard, because of privacy reasons I have been unable to obtain a full list either of those foreign faculty denied visas to teach on the West Bank or those whose visa renewals have been denied. And the reasons for visa denials are typically not public either in Israel or in other countries. As noted above, in 2019 the Israeli NGO Adalah did join with Al-Haq, a Palestinian human rights group that is a leader in BDS campaigns (with links to the Popular Front for the Liberation of Palestine),[49] to mount a legal challenge regarding four visiting faculty at Birzeit who encountered visa problems and to publicize their names: Haneen Adi, Rana Barakat, Rania Jawad, and Omar Tesdell. *Inside Higher Education* published a news story focusing on a fifth, Roger Heacock, who had taught at Birzeit for thirty-some years before being blocked from passing over the Allenby bridge from Jordan into the West Bank (Redden). Adalah attorney and Deputy General Director Sawsan Zaher protested that the fact of the occupation "does not cancel the academic freedom of universities in Palestine to decide and determine who will be brought to teach and for what time and what kind of research" (Redden). Academic freedom does give universities the right of faculty selection, but, once again, it does not give universities visa-granting power. Some appear to believe a university offer alone should settle the matter, which is not reasonable. On the other hand, published government guidelines should make it clear what criteria are in play. As Israeli government officials confirmed to me, of the five individuals named above, two currently have visas, and two others had not completed the bureaucratic process at the time their entry was denied.[50]

---

49. See NGO Monitor's report on Al-Haq for further background.

50. It is worth noting that, so far as I know, Birzeit has neither updated nor corrected its news release, and no news outlet has corrected its account either.

The factual record does not support Birzeit's claim that "Israel has escalated what can only be understood as a policy whose ultimate goal is the elimination of any international faculty presence at Palestinian universities."

The common complaint by BDS advocates about foreign teaching faculty repeatedly compelled to leave the West Bank to apply for a new tourist visa every three months misrepresents the reality. The obvious question to ask is why some faculty members choose to teach without applying for the longer visa beforehand. No one I consulted knew whether there is an informal network advising people to teach on three-month tourist visas or whether Palestinian institutions are giving that advice. Of course in Israel, as in the US and elsewhere, some simply choose to break the law and overstay their visas. Some then decide to apply for a legal visa; it should be no surprise that the odds of success at that point are small to nonexistent.

Many countries, we should recognize, have visa restrictions comparable to those Israel has historically applied. Australia, for example, in 2014 amended Section 501 of its 1958 Migration Act to give the Minister for Home Affairs the power to cancel the visa of a person who would "incite discord in the Australian community" or represent a danger to a segment of the community (Australian Government). Canada's Minister of Immigration has the authority to deny temporary residence to anyone who "incite[s] hatred that is likely to lead to violence against a specific group" or makes public statements or distributes website materials that "promote or glorify terrorist violence" (Government of Canada). France can refuse entry to anyone who would represent a threat to public order. The US has frequently exercised much broader authority to bar entry to foreign faculty with offers of teaching appointments when a given administration apparently finds the individual's political views offensive. The American Association of University Professors has more than once fought those decisions, as it did when Tariq Ramadan was prevented from taking up an offer for a tenured position at Notre Dame, but not necessarily successfully. Of course an unwarranted visa denial by the US does not justify one by Israel; nor, however, is it either ethical or responsible to pretend that Israel's practices are unique. Indeed, the largest travel restriction policies by far are elsewhere. As of 2020, in Turkey "thousands of university personnel accused of affiliations disfavored by the state and linked to a July 2016 coup attempt remain fired, barred from civil service employment, and unable to leave the country, as per a series of State of Emergency decrees" (Scholars at Risk 2019, 25).[51] Meanwhile, China detains as many as a million members of its Uyghur community, including many Uyghur scholars and students, in forced reeducation camps, subject to psychological coercion and barred from travel.

---

51. Scholars at Risk issues detailed, well-researched reports on countries like China, Iran, and Turkey that massively abridge academic freedom. I find those reports consistently reliable, as are their thorough analyses of individual violations. Less reliable are their brief expressions of concern about single incidents where context is lacking and their sometimes implicit conclusions are not supported by a full airing of the facts.

CONCLUSION

This essay has tracked violent actions that responsible stakeholders both within and without the higher education and public communities should condemn. The more vexing question for Palestinian universities, the Palestinian Authority, Israel itself, and the interested international community remains how to distinguish between valid political expression protected by academic freedom and political expression or political activity devoted to terrorist recruitment or incitement to violence. Moreover, as we are all learning, a vast amount of terrorist incitement on the internet and on social media is outside the direct control of Israel, the PA, or anyone else. That does not, however, eliminate the need to investigate instances of face-to-face recruitment and incitement, either on campus or elsewhere. And certainly internet platforms that give users the opportunity to livestream terrorist attacks should be shut down. Moreover, private companies like Facebook that own and maintain their platform can block the dissemination of hate speech, including that posted by Palestinians, if they choose to do so. Advertisers can withdraw ads from platforms like Facebook that have been willing to post anti-Semitic or racist content in order to press them to reform their policies. The text and illustrations in *Not in Kansas Anymore* document Facebook's willingness to post anti-Semitic text and images. The IDF and terrorist groups, it should be noted, have been engaged in cyber warfare for a generation (Amer "Hamas's cyber battalions"). Hamas put bomb-making directions online in 2002 (Rense) and successfully recruited students to use the information. There needs to be ongoing monitoring of terrorist, racist, and anti-Semitic content on less well known platforms like those documented by Britain's Community Security Trust, among them BitChute, Telegram, Gab, and 4chan.

Writing before the First Intifada in his untranslated 1986 Arabic language book on Palestinian higher education, Birzeit political scientist and former Minister of Higher Education Ali Jarbawi could argue that "the presence of politicized elements within the universities has never demonstrated that the institutions as a whole are politicized" (58).[52] One can still argue that not every class session in every course is engaged with political issues, but the larger claim became unsustainable in the course of the First Intifada and wholly detached from reality once university students became involved in suicide bombings and campus communities began celebrating terrorism (Figs. 1, 3, 4, 8, 9, 10, 11, 12, 13).

A February 20, 1987 *Al-Fajir* editorial could complain that Israelis "want Palestinian students to be passive toward the events that take place around them. They want impotent and politically inactive students." Whatever some Israelis might have wished, it was soon clear that hope would not be realized. "What kind of people will the Palestinian graduates be," the editorial continued, "if they are not allowed to think and express their own and their people's political aspirations?" Yet faculty and students throughout the world are able to voice their political aspirations at length without crossing a line into violence or permitting their universities to become terrorist incitement centers. Writing in his 1987 essay "Politics and Relevance in Palestinian Higher Education," Antony Sullivan argued that "Palestinians understandably look to their institutions of higher learning to produce the leadership that will resist further Israeli settlement in the Occupied Territories, discourage continued Israeli seizure of Palestinian land and water resources, and challenge the arrest and imprisonment of Palestinian nationalists by the Israeli occupation authorities." My own view is that all these goals can be advocated and pursued by nonviolent political action and civil disobedience. Yet by now, two decades into the twenty-first century, a Palestinian higher education commitment to nonviolence would amount to a wholesale transformation of its actual mission.

Meanwhile, tolerance for political expression among Palestinian factions may well be diminishing. In an April 2019 story, Israeli-Palestinian journalist Khaled Abu Toameh complained that "Palestinian students

---

52. The passage is translated in Antony Sullivan's "Politics and Relevance in Palestinian Higher Education."

are being targeted because of their political affiliations and not because of any crime that they committed" ("Targets Students"). His complaint was not against the Israelis: "In recent weeks, the PA has been waging a campaign of arrests and intimidation against Palestinian students at some of the West Bank universities." The An-Najah administration joined in, issuing "a directive banning the Islamic Bloc student list from carrying out any activities on campus." The PA reinforced the campaign by arresting two students. An-Najah meanwhile defended its action by emphasizing that it was also banning Fatah political activities. Interestingly, the administration added that "tensions on campus only escalated after Hamas's recent brutal crackdown on Fatah supporters in the Gaza Strip." Fatah reported that Hamas broke the arms and legs of dozens of Fatah protestors in Gaza. As they have been doing for over a decade, "the Palestinian Authority and Hamas are busy beating up each other's supporters." One takeaway from such stories is that reactive Palestinian suppression of dissent can take place across the divide between Gaza and the West Bank. But the deeper lesson once again is that political expression and violence are often indistinguishable in the area. No one with policy or policing responsibilities, whether Israeli or Palestinian, has an easy job. We must consider the conflicting histories, values, interests, risks, and realities carefully before making judgments about the decisions either universities or political authorities make.

From 2017 through 2020 overall, Hamas and PA patience with their long-standing political opponents appeared to be wearing ever more thin. News headlines such as "Hamas-Fatah bitter split plays out in West Bank universities" (Melhem), "Hamas police violently suppress Gaza student protest" (Toameh), and "Palestinian Authority Targets Students" (Toameh) highlighted the focus on universities as key sites to enact political hostilities. But a relatively new development was repeated assertions by the parties themselves that forces in Gaza and the West Bank were effectively carrying out reprisals for political repression in each other's territory. Human Rights Watch issued a 2018 report, "Two Authorities, One Way, Zero Dissent: Arbitrary Arrest and Torture Under the Palestinian Authority and Hamas." Here is one paragraph from their summary:

Palestinian authorities closely monitor criticism of the PA at universities. In January 2017, PA forces detained Fares Jbour, an electrical engineering student in Hebron, and questioned him about his participation in a book drive organized by the Hamas-affiliated Islamic Bloc on campus. Jbour told Human Rights Watch that PA forces had arrested him five previous times over his peaceful activities with the bloc, and said that prosecutors charged him with "weapons possession," "forming militias," "heading an armed gang," and "money laundering," but released him without referring him to court. In February 2017, Hamas police held Youssef Omar, who teaches history at Al-Aqsa University in Gaza, along with four other professors, apparently over their activism with the union of university employees, which opposed Hamas' attempt to appoint a new university president without consulting the PA.

The irony for those in the West, as Toameh points out in his 2019 article, is that "While the Palestinian Authority and Hamas are busy beating up each other's supporters, 'pro-Palestinian' activists on US and Canadian university campuses are busy blaming Israel for Palestinian woes." Of course blaming Israel for all Palestinian-on-Palestinian violence deprives Palestinians of all power of choice in their actions. Would they suddenly be invested with moral agency if the occupation ended? If violence is simply an involuntary reaction to the occupation, there are no limits to the actions for which responsibility can be disavowed, though area political authorities are as likely as Israel to be blamed by participants. When Islamic Bloc students at Birzeit are "charged with serious crimes such as sectarian violence, libel, defamation, or even receiving funds from illicit parties or possessing weapons" they claim the accusations "are mostly fabricated" (Melhem).

Meanwhile, students themselves continue to enact these hostilities. In reaction to a December 17, 2018, Birzeit University brawl between the Hamas and Fatah student blocs, the school's assistant president, Aziz Shwayka, "urged all parties to 'stop disrupting academic life and consider the university space a sacred one that is not to be desecrated'" (Melhem). Such an appeal might suffice in other countries, but it has no chance of success in Gaza or the West Bank. As this essay has demonstrated, Palestinian universities are not and have never been sacred spaces maintained above the fray. Given a settlement of all internal and external conflicts, that might change over a generation or two, but hostility toward Israel would have to dissipate substantially (or at least see its violent impulses lose social support) to make that happen. So long as combined political/religious opposition to the very existence of a Jewish state remains the controlling Palestinian conviction, these universities will continue to abridge academic freedom.

Indeed, there is one political subject quite free of threat or intimidation—criticism of the Jewish state. Palestinian academics and the general public alike are free to inveigh against Israel relentlessly. As Bassam Tawil, a scholar based in the Middle East, wrote in July 2018, "Palestinians are permitted to badmouth Israel and the US—but that is where their 'freedom of speech' ends. Let a Palestinian utter a bad word about his leaders—he will find himself (or herself) behind bars." He adds that "In recent weeks, the PA's campaign against its political critics reached several Palestinian university campuses, where scores of students have been arrested or summoned for interrogation. The PA's tough security measures at university campuses are seen by Palestinians in the context of the PA leadership's ongoing effort to silence and intimidate its critics and political rivals." His conclusion is severe: "By targeting Palestinian journalists and university students, the Palestinian Authority shows that it has turned the territories under its control into a dictatorship that systematically grinds public freedoms into the ground." Advocacy for Hamas and Islamic Jihad, on the other hand, are tracked to the degree possible by both Israel and the PA, but academic freedom prevails where faulting Israel is concerned.

As Scholars at Risk details in its annual reports, at the same time, we continue to see horrific campus-related assaults abridging academic freedom elsewhere in the world that dwarf anything that has happened on the West Bank. On January 15, 2013, two explosions at Aleppo University in Syria killed at least 82 people and injured twice that number. In September 2014, 43 students at Mexico's Raúl Isidro Burgos Rural Teacher's College of Ayotzinpa were apparently kidnapped before being "disappeared." The local narcotics gang Guerreros Unidos had been enlisted by local authorities to carry out the murders. On April 2, 2015, gunmen from the Somali militant group Al Shabaab invaded Kenya's Garissa University College, where they killed 142 students and several others. On October 24, 2016, militants attacked Pakistan's Balochistan Police College in Quetta, killing at least 61 people, most of them students. This entire essay could be filled with accounts of assaults producing smaller numbers of campus fatalities. Among the factors that distinguish Palestinian violence from that occurring in a number of other geographical areas are, first of all, its duration over several decades; second, the multiple vectors through which it operates; third, the combination of religion and politics at stake; fourth, the mix of state and nonstate actors responsible; and fifth, the prevalence of university student participation. The combination of all these elements makes the relevant violence and threat notably intractable.

The place where academic freedom is ultimately tested is over free expression about politics and religion. It is a test that even democratic countries struggle to pass, especially when wartime political expression is at issue. During and after World War I, during World War II, and during the McCarthy period of the 1950s, the United States was willing to compromise or set aside its constitutional guarantees for self-expression. Like other Americans, faculty members sometimes lost their jobs as a result. Some Americans faced prison. During wartime, faculty members who express controversial opinions can expect to face severe criticism from colleagues, politicians, and members of the public. The most important question is whether they face sanctions as a result. During Operation Protective Edge in 2014, faculty members in Israel who criticized the war were excoriated by conservative politicians and members of the public. But they did not lose their jobs, and they did not go to jail. Israel has an exceptionally good record of honoring academic freedom within its pre-1967 boundaries. There have been some challenges to political expression by Arab student citizens in Israel proper, but, once again, sanctions have generally been avoided.

Israel confronted extraordinary challenges during the wave of suicide bombings that accompanied the Second Intifada from 2000 to 2005. We should remember that Hebrew University of Jerusalem's Mount Scopus campus endured a suicide bombing on July 31, 2002. The attack, which took place in the Student Center cafeteria during lunchtime, killed nine people, among them five American students, and injured about 100 others. Seven died immediately, while two others succumbed to their wounds in the following weeks. Hamas took credit for the attack (Military Wikia). From 2000 to 2005, there were 138 suicide bombings in Israel, along with numerous other terror attacks. Decisions about how to handle violence and incitement to violence became urgent as a result. Both Israel and the Palestinian Authority have felt similar pressures during the wave of knife and automotive attacks that began in the fall of 2015. Hamas is now focused on planting explosives and detonating them after the perpetrator leaves the scene, but that is hardly a comforting difference from suicide bombing.

In any case, as I have shown and repeatedly emphasized, the most serious threats to academic freedom in Gaza and the West Bank come from Palestinian society itself. The BDS movement in the United States has focused its moral outrage on such matters as foreign faculty members being denied entry to teach in the West Bank, though some simply face delayed entry by Israeli authorities. Actual denials can be appealed to Israeli courts. Does not the widespread, overt Palestinian hostility toward divergent political and religious views—accompanied by the willingness to punish students and faculty for holding them—represent a constant assault on academic freedom? Are not Palestinian attempts to kill Mohammed Dajani and Abdul Sattar Qassem for their politically incorrect speech exceptionally serious? Do not the gangs of student enforcers trained by Hamas to intimidate, harass, and assault dissident faculty members represent a great threat to academic freedom? There is little hope for dialogue with those unwilling to answer these questions in the affirmative.

Indeed, there is little evidence that anti-Zionist faculty members, once firmly committed to the cause, would agree to consider the evidence gathered here. A September 2015 boycott resolution promoted by Historians Against the War (HAW), an interest group within the American Historical Association (AHA), does not even mention Hamas, despite complaining about Israel's actions in Gaza. Neither in the resolution nor in thirty additional pages of documentation is there any acknowledgment that Hamas's unprovoked rocket attacks on Israeli civilians mandated an Israeli response (Gluck). The resolution was resubmitted again in 2019, once again without referencing Hamas's extensive violations of academic freedom with HAW renamed H-PAD (Historians for Peace and Democracy). It was defeated again at the January 2020 annual AHA meeting. Israel was once again the lone cul-prit. The threats to academic freedom from Palestinian on Palestinian violence received no acknowledgement in H-PAD's documents or in those by boycott proponents in the Modern Language Association and other faculty groups. The 2019 renewal of HAW's project of weapon-izing ignorance and misinformation did, however, include another measure of disinformation. Even though the traditional route for travel abroad from Gaza through Cairo to universities elsewhere was revived when Egypt reopened the Rafah crossing on Gaza's southern border in February 2019, H-PAD chose not to mention that fact in the October resubmission.

Does that mean there is no hope? Not quite. As I detail in *Israel Denial*, think tanks in Israel and the US have devised solutions to the practical challenges peace presents. And there is a story about one small seminar at a Palestinian University, admittedly taught by two excep-tional faculty members, that shows us a different direction. As Carlos Fraenkel (McGill University) remarks in discussing a remarkable philos-ophy seminar he co-taught with Sari Nusseibeh at Al-Quds University in East Jerusalem in 2006, "although stereotypes and prejudices are probably not dissolved, they are at least suspended during personal con-versation" (23). There were only eight students in the class, but one of them was allied with Hamas. We are in a very different world. Fraenkel points out that he never sees Nusseibeh "without his bodyguards. They inspect the classroom before he comes in and guard the door during class" (9). Twenty years after the account of the harrowing, near lethal assault that opened this paper, the threat environment does not appear to have changed. As a university president, however, Nusseibeh now has access to bodyguards, not a service an ordinary faculty member is likely to have available. The reality outside the seminar room is never too far away; indeed, its intrusion is invited:

> We go through some standard examples from the Israeli-Palestinian conflict, where things were done that the agents claimed to be just and religiously motivated, but whose justice is obviously doubtful: from Baruch Goldstein's 1994 massacre of Palestinians in Hebron

> and the assassination of Yitzhak Rabin by Yigal Amir in 1995, to the 2002 suicide bombing at Rehavia's Café Moment where I'd often gone for dinner or drinks as a graduate student . . . . Although most of the students accept the idea that it is important to examine religious notions in a Socratic manner, their commitment to the truth of Islam leaves no room for confusion . . . . During a break Bisma shows photos in class, some of which I and the other men are not allowed to see because she appears in them without the veil. (Fraenkel 14, 15, 19-20)

Fraenkel may be overly optimistic. "Even if the Middle East isn't yet ready to be saved," he writes, "philosophy can make an important contribution—through rational arguments that can be understood and evaluated without regard to religious or national commitments" (28). It is striking that the seminar can compare and contrast Palestinian and Israeli violence, apparently somewhat dispassionately. Fraenkel's anecdote holds out the possibility that reason could replace rage as a psychological and social resource, but whether the lesson learned would shape how any of the students would conduct themselves in a factional political meeting is impossible to say. We cannot know if the intellectual openness that prevailed in the seminar carried over into more partisan settings. Of course real change would require a critical mass of people who think differently and communities willing to act on that basis. Nonetheless, that is the part of the difference education is supposed to make in our lives. Occasionally it does.

Not in Kansas Anymore has a title that is a multivalent provocation—partly satiric, partly a deliberate challenge, partly a coldly factual statement about the differences the essay challenges the reader to recognize. All these variations are focused on the reader and on the widespread assumptions that block understanding. "A university is a university is a university" only serves as a reliable motto if the repetition calls the stability of the object it invokes into question. In the passage from here to there, from Kansas to Ramallah, we pass from one compromised value system to another very different one, and the transformation is not a welcome one. Academic freedom no longer applies. Dorothy figured out that something had changed; most in the West have not yet done so.

CODA

Palestinian universities often declare their support for academic freedom. In September 2016, I wrote to a distinguished West Bank Palestinian faculty member to ask whether his or any other Palestinian university had adopted formal regulations about academic freedom. His answer: "I do not think any Palestinian university has such code. Maybe foreign universities should pressure them to have one."

Finally, after the evidence supplied in the foregoing pages, perhaps I can end with a reflection on my cover. The title, as noted, borrows a phrase from Dorothy's famous remark to her dog in *The Wizard of Oz:* "Toto, I've a feeling we're not in Kansas anymore." The cover alludes to the movie version with a background image of a midwestern tornado. The insert photo depicts what a Palestinian university looks like from an uninformed Western vantage point. It shows a central square at An-Najah University in Nablus, with the campus as a conventionally neutral and architecturally attractive space, one with doorways to instruction and space for public gatherings. But that is only half the story, the other half consisting of compromised academic freedom, Palestinian-on-Palestinian violence, and student involvement in terrorism.

REFERENCES[53]

Abaza, Jihad, "Palestinian Authority forces arrest students affiliated with Hamas," *Daily News* (May 8, 2015), online at http://www.dailynewsegypt.com/2015/05/08/258063/.

Abou-dagga, Prof. Sanaa I, "Quality Assurance in the Palestinian Higher Education Institutions," Islamic University (October 2012), online at http://site.iugaza.edu.ps/sdagga/files/QA-at-IUG-10-9-2012.pdf.

Abu-Amr, Ziad. *Islamic Fundamentalism in the West Bank and Gaza: Muslim Brotherhood and Islamic Jihad.* Bloomington: Indiana University Press, 1994.

Abu Lughod, Ibrahim, "Palestinian Higher Education: National Identity, Liberation, and Globalization," *Boundary* 2 27:1 (2000), 75–95.

Abudheir, Farid. *Palestinian University Students' Exposure to Islamic Websites: An-Najah and Birzeit Universities as Examples.* Saarbrücken, Germany: Noor Publishing, 2016.

Academic Freedom Monitor, "Incident Report: Birzeit University, May 7, 2015," *Scholars at Risk*, online at http://monitoring.academicfreedom.info/node/688.

Adalah, "Birzeit University faculty members available for media interviews" (July 7, 2019), online at https://www.adalah.org/en/content/view/9765.

Aghazarian, Albert, "Early Supporters." In Ida Audeh, ed. *Birzeit University: The Story of a National Institution*, p. 78.

Ahronheim, Anna, "Shin Bet Arrests Reveal Gaza-Turkey-West Bank Money Chain," *The Jerusalem Post* (May 3, 2018), online at https://www.jpost.com/Arab-Israeli-Conflict/Israel-arrests-Hamas-agents-smuggling-cash-for-university-terror-activity-553379.

---

53. In order not to overwhelm this bibliography, I have not listed the many studies of Israeli-Palestinian and area history that I have consulted for my four books on the subject. Those bibliographies can be reviewed in the books themselves. I should also point out that this is not a recommended list of readings. I draw on books and essays here with a wide range of political viewpoints. A number of them are unreservedly hostile toward Israel. Thus Sam Abd Al-Qadir Alfoqahaa of An-Najah University includes in an overview of Palestinian education the claim that Israel is "trying to mislead the world to believe that Palestinians do not deserve to live" (35). I do not accept that claim, but I believe he is well positioned to testify that particular courses are taught in Palestinian universities. Thus often a politically biased essay will have some useful factual information and analysis.

Alfoqahaa, Sam Abd Al-Qadir, "Economics of Higher Education under Occupation," *Journal of Arts & Humanities* 4:10 (2015), 25-43.

Alexander, Neta, "The Palestinian Professor Who Took Students on Auschwitz Trip and Paid a Heavy Price," *Haaretz* (September 15, 2016), online at http://www.haaretz.com/israel-news/.premium-1.742212.

Alliance for Academic Freedom, "Academic Freedom and Educational Opportunity Worldwide: A White Paper from the Alliance for Academic Freedom" (December 15, 2019), online at https://thirdnarrative.org/wp-content/uploads/2019/12/Academic-Freedom-Worldwide-for-2020-Final.pdf.

Alliance for Academic Freedom, "Two Flawed Resolutions: Errors, Misrepresentations, and Omissions in the Resolutions Before the AHA" (December 17, 2019), online at https://thirdnarrative.org/wp-content/uploads/2019/12/Errors-and-Omissions-2020-final.pdf.

Amayreh, Khalid, "PA Must Stop Persecuting Abdul Sattar Qassem," Palestinian Information Center (January 9, 2011), online at http://english.palinfo.com/site/pages/details.aspx?itemid=67668.

Amer, Adnan Abu, "Hamas' cyber battalions take on Israel," *Al-Monitor* (July 29, 2015), online at www.al-monitor.com/pulse/originals/2015/07/.

_____, "How Hamas Scored a Win in West Bank Student Elections," *Al-Monitor* (May 5, 2016), available at http://www.al-monitor.com/pulse/originals/2016/05/hamas-birzeit-university-elections-winning-indications.html.

_____, "The PA is targeting Hamas' student body in the West Bank," *Middle East Monitor* (April 8, 2019), online at https://www.middleeastmonitor.com/20190408-the-pa-is-targeting-hamas-student-body-in-the-west-bank/.

Amnesty International, "Palestinian Authority: Justice must not be discarded" (November 8, 2001), online at https://www.amnesty.org/download/Documents/128000/mde210232001en.pdf.

_____, "State of Palestine: Alarming attack on Freedom of Expression" (August 23, 2017), online at https://www.amnesty.org/en/documents/mde15/6983/2017/en/.

_____, "Palestine: Dangerous escalation in attacks on freedom of expression" (August 23, 2017), online at https://www.amnesty.org/en/latest/news/2017/08/palestine-dangerous-escalation-in-attacks-on-freedom-of-expression/.

Anabtawi, Samir N. *Palestinian Higher Education in the West Bank and Gaza.* London: Routledge & Kegan Paul, 1986.

Aronson, Geoffrey. *Israel, Palestinians and the Intifada: Creating Facts on the West Bank.* NY: Kegan Paul International, 1990.

Arutz Sheva Staff, "'Don't die a natural death—die as a terrorist!'" *Arutz Sheva* (October 27, 2016), online at https://www.israelnationalnews.com/News/News.aspx/219444.

Audeh, Ida. ed. *Birzeit University: The Story of a National Institution*. Birzeit, Palestine: Birzeit University Publications, 2010.

Australian Government Federal Register of Legislation, "Migration Act 1958" (December 2017), online at https://www.legislation.gov.au/Details/C2017C00384.

Awajneh, Ahlam Mustafa Hasan, Suhair ulaiman Mohammed Sabbah, and Inas Aref Saleh Naserr, "Concepts and Role of Faculty in the Palestinian Universities in the Light of Knowledge Economy," *World Journal of Education* 7:6 (2017), 80–89.

Baramki, Gabi. *Peaceful Resistance: Building a Palestinian University Under Occupation*. Foreword by Jimmy Carter. London: Pluto Press, 2010.

Beaumont, Peter, "Palestinians kill suspected collaborators," *The Guardian* (April 1, 2002), online at https://www.theguardian.com/world/2002/apr/02/israel.

Bennet, James, "Israel Closes Two Universities in Hebron as Terrorist Havens," *The New York Times* (January 16, 2003), online at https://www.nytimes.com/2003/01/16/world/israel-closes-two-universities-in-hebron-as-terrorist-havens.html.

Bennett, Andrew Mark, "JVP's Anti-Semitic Obsession with Jewish Power," *The Forward* (January 9, 2018), online at https://forward.com/opinion/391783/jvps-anti-semitic-obsession-with-jewish-power/.

Birzeit University Office of Public Relations. *The Criminalization of Education, Academic Freedom, and Human Rights at Birzeit University During the Palestinian Uprising*. Birzeit, Palestine: Birzeit University, 1989.

Birzeit University, "UPDATE: Birzeit University continues to lose international faculty as Israel persists in discriminatory policy" (November 14, 2019), online at https://www.birzeit.edu/en/news/update-birzeit-university-continues-lose-international-faculty-israel-persists-discriminatory.

Blumenthal, Itay, "West Bank students indicted for links with Hamas," *Ynet News* (March 10, 2018), online at https://www.ynetnews.com/articles/0,7340,L-5363034,00.html.

Braunschweiger, Amy, "Interview: How Palestinian Authorities Crush Dissent," *Human Rights Watch* (October 23, 2018), online at https://www.hrw.org/news/2018/10/23/interview-how-palestinian-authorities-crush-dissent.

Brown, Larisa, and Flora Drury, "Hamas executed Palestinian 'collaborators' with AK-47s in front of hundreds of spectators including children for 'assisting Israel' during last Gaza conflict, reveals Amnesty International," *Daily Mail* (May 27, 2015), online at http://www.dailymail.co.uk/news/ article-3098254/Hamas-executed-Palestinian-collaborators-AK-47s-hundreds-spectators-including-children-assisting-Israel-Gaza-conflict-reveals-Amnesty-International.html.

Bruhn, Christa, "Higher Education as Empowerment: The Case of Palestinian Universities," *American Behavioral Scientist* 49:8 (April 2006), 1125-1142.

B'Tselem, "Harm to Palestinians suspected of collaborating with Israel" (January 1, 2011), online at https://www.btselem.org/collaboration.

Butler, Judith, "Israel/Palestine and the Paradox of Academic Freedom," *Radical Philosophy* 135 (Jan/Feb 2006), online at https://www. radicalphilosophy.com/article/israelpalestine-and-the-paradoxes-of-academic-freedom.

_____, "Exercising Rights: Academic Freedom and Boycott Politics." In Akeel Bilgami and Jonathan R. Cole, eds. *Who's Afraid of Academic Freedom*. NY: Columbia University Press, 2015, pp. 293-315.

California Faculty Association, "Resolution in Defense of Academic Freedom for Professor Abdulhadi" (2017), online at https://www.calfac.org/ item/resolution-defense-academic-freedom-professor-abdulhadi-0.

Caschetta, A.J., "In Criticizing Israel, MESA Ignores Terror Threats on Palestinian Campuses." *The Tower* (February 5, 2019), online at http://www. thetower.org/7150-in-criticizing-israel-mesa-ignores-terror-threats-on-palestinian-campuses/.

Cemmel, James, "Academic Freedom International Study: Palestine" (May 2009), University and College Union/Education International.

Cambanis, Thanissis. "Hamas U," *Boston Globe* (February 28, 2010), online at http://archive.boston.com/bostonglobe/ideas/articles/2010/02/28/ hamas_u/?page=4.

Carter, Jimmy, "Foreword." In Gadi Baramki, *Peaceful Resistance: Building a Palestinian University Under Occupation*, ix.

Chosak, Jamie, and Julie Sawyer, "Hamas's Tactics: Lessons from Recent Attacks," *The Washington Institute* (October 19, 2005), online at https:// www.washingtoninstitute.org/policy-analysis/view/hamass-tactics-lessons-from-recent-attacks.

CNN, "8 Dead as Gaza battle rages" (February 2, 2007), online at http:// www.cnn.com/2007/WORLD/meast/02/02/israel.palestinians/index.html.

Cohen, Gili, "Hamas Cell Operating in Abu Dis Planned Suicide Attacks in Israel, Says Shin Bet," *Haaretz* (December 23, 2015), online at http://www. haaretz.com/israel-news/.premium-1.693420.

_____, "Palestinian Who Murdered Rabbi Michael Mark Killed in West Bank Clashes, Shin Bet Confirms," *Haaretz* (July 27, 2016), online at https://www.haaretz.com/israel-news/palestinian-who-murdered-michael-mark-killed-shin-bet-says-1.5416503.

Cohen, Shimon, "Al Quds University unveils Christmas 'martyr tree'" *Arutz Sheva* (December 9, 2015), online at www.israelnationalnews.com/News/News.aspx/204624.

Columbia University *Students for Justice in Palestine & Columbia/Barnard Jewish Voice for Peace*, "New Dual Degree Program Puts Columbia's Academic Integrity at Risk" (December 9, 2019), online at https://docs.google.com/document/d/1d4hNMFmjeywXvV0n8THv2KG92U4VlvwfMiGhpP-N_cw/edit.

Community Security Trust. *Hate Fuel: the hidden online world that fuels far right terror* (London, 2020).

Dajani, Mohammed "Why Palestinians Should Support 'Normalization with Israel," *Haaretz* (September 13, 2016), online at https://www.washingtoninstitute.org/fikraforum/view/why-palestinians-should-support-normalization-with-israel.

Dajani, Mohammed Daoudi and Robert Satloff, "Why Palestinians Should Learn about the Holocaust," *New York Times* (March 29, 2011), online at http://www.nytimes.com/2011/03/30/opinion/30iht-edsatloff30.html?_r=0.

Daragmi, Alaa, "Pro Hamas Bloc Wins Birzeit University Student Elections for 4th Year in Row," *The Palestine Chronicle* (May 10, 2018), online at https://www.palestinechronicle.com/pro-hamas-bloc-wins-birzeit-university-student-elections-for-4th-year-in-row-video/.

Dudkevitch, Margot, "Netanya wedding hall bombing foiled," *The Jerusalem Post* (July 28, 2004).

El-Khodary, Taghreed, "Hamas and Fatah Supporters Clash at Gaza University," *New York Times* (April 1, 2008), online at https://www.nytimes.com/2008/04/01/world/middleeast/01mideast.html.

Elman, Miriam, "Jewish Voice for Peace—'Jew Washing' the anti-Israel movement," *Legal Insurrection* (July 12, 2015), online at https://legalinsurrection.com/2015/07/jewish-voice-for-peace-jew-washing-the-anti-israel-movement/.

_____, "Never forget: Sbarro Pizzeria Massacre, Jerusalem, Aug. 9, 2001," *Legal Insurrection* (August 9, 2015), online at https://legalinsurrection.com/2016/08/never-forget-sbarro-pizzeria-massacre-jerusalem-aug-9-2001/.

Emerson, Steve, "Israel Arrests Hamas-Linked Cell in Bomb Plots," *Newsmax* (April 28, 2020).

Epstein, Nadine, "Mohammed Dajani Daoudi: Evolution of a Moderate," *Moment* (July/August 2014) 23-59.

Essa, Azad, "Students accuse Columbia University of 'importing racism' from Israel," *Middle East Eye* (December 11, 2019), online at https://www.middleeasteye.net/news/students-accuse-columbia-university-importing-racism-israel.

Estrin, Daniel, and Abu Bakr Bashir, "'I Want To Get The Hell Out Of Here': Thousands Of Palestinians Are Leaving Gaza'" *NPR* (July 4, 2019), online at https://www.npr.org/2019/07/04/733487137/i-want-to-get-the-hell-out-of-here-thousands-of-palestinians-are-leaving-gaza.

Eurasia Review, "Gaza: Calls to Stop Suppressing Peaceful Protests" (March 19, 2011), online at https://www.eurasiareview.com/19032011-gaza-calls-to-stop-suppressing-peaceful-protests/.

European Commission (TEMPUS), "Higher Education in the Occupied Palestinian Territory," (2012), online at https://www.kooperation-international.de/fileadmin/redaktion/doc/Palaestina_Tempus2012_Higher_edu_system_Pal.pdf.

Fasheh, Munir, "The Intimate Relationship between Birzeit and Its Larger Context." In Ida Audeh, ed. *Birzeit University: The Story of a National Institution*, pp. 31-33.

Finkelstein, Norman G. *Gaza: An Inquest Into Its Martyrdom*. Berkeley: University of California Press, 2018.

Fraenkel, Carlos. *Teaching Plato in Palestine: Philosophy in a Divided World*. Princeton: Princeton University Press, 2015.

Franks, Lynne Rosengrant. *Israel and the Occupied Territories: A Study of the Educational Systems of Israel and the Occupied Territories and a Guide to the Academic Placement of Students in Educational Institutions in the United States*. Washington, DC: United States Information Agency, 1987.

Freedom House, "Freedom of the Press—Israel" (2016), online at https://freedomhouse.org/report/freedom-press/2016/israel.

_____, "Freedom of the Press—West Bank and Gaza Strip" (2017), online at https://freedomhouse.org/report/freedom-press/2015/west-bank-and-gaza-strip.

_____, "Freedom in the World—Gaza Strip" (2019), online at https://freedomhouse.org/report/freedom-world/2019/gaza-strip.

_____, "Freedom in the World—Israel" (2019), online at https://freedomhouse.org/report/freedom-world/2019/israel.

_____, "Freedom in the World—West Bank" (2019), online at https://freedomhouse.org/report/freedom-world/2019/west-bank.

Frommer, Rachel, "Promotion of Terrorism Against Israel at Birzeit U Highlighted in Profile of Palestinian Institution of Higher Learning" *The Algemeiner* (March 5, 2017), online at https://www.algemeiner. com/2017/03/05/promotion-of-terrorism-against-israel-at-birzeit-u-highlighted-in-profile-of-palestinian-institution-of-higher-learning/.

Fulbright, Alexander, "In daylight campus raid, undercover commandos nab West Bank student leader," *Times of Israel* (March 7, 2018), online at https://www.timesofisrael.com/in-daylight-campus-raid-undercover-commandos-nab-west-bank-student-leader/.

Gancman, Lee, "Al-Quds University puts up martyr-themed Christmas tree," *The Times of Israel* (December 4, 2015), online at https://www. timesofisrael.com/al-quds-university-puts-up-martyr-themed-christmas-tree/.

Gavison, Ruth, and Yehoshua Kolodny, David Kretchmer, Eliezar Rabinovitch, and Menahem Yari, "Report on the Condition of Universities in the Occupied Territories." Reprinted in Gabi Baramki, *Peaceful Resistance*, pp.183-206.

Gerner, Deborah J. and Philip A. Schrodt, "Into the New Millennium: Challenges Facing Palestinian Higher Education in the Twenty-First Century," *Arab Studies Quarterly* 21:4 (1999), 1934.

Gerstman, David, "Pro-Israel Scholars Counter Move by Major US Academic Association to Boycott Israel," *Algemeiner* (August 16, 2019), online at https://www.algemeiner.com/2019/08/16/pro-israel-scholars-counter-move-by-major-us-academic-association-to-boycott-israel/.

_____, "Opposition Grows to Pro-BDS Resolution Set to Be Voted on by Major Academic Association," *Algemeiner* (July 22, 2019), online at https://www.algemeiner.com/2019/07/22/opposition-grows-to-pro-bds-resolution-set-to-be-voted-on-by-major-academic-association/.

_____, "Major US Academic Association Votes Down Resolution to Boycott Israel," *Algemeiner* (August 12, 2019), online at https://www. algemeiner.com/2019/08/12/major-academic-association-votes-down-bds-resolution/

Ghorbiah, Elia, "Hamas wins student elections at Birzeit University for third year," *Middle East Eye* (May 11, 2017), online at https://www.middleeasteye. net/news/hamas-wins-student-elections-birzeit-university-third-year.

GISHA, "Gaza's Academic Sector" (Tel Aviv: September 2016).

_____, "Status of Authorizations: Changes to Israel's criteria on movement of people to and from the Gaza Strip," GISHA, September 2019, online at https://gisha.org/UserFiles/File/LegalDocuments/Changes_to_status_of_authorization_EN.pdf

Gluck, Sherna Berger, "Impediments to Education in the Occupied Territories" (September 2015), Historians Against the War, online at https://www.usacbi.org/wp/wp-content/uploads/2013/11/ACIMPED.pdf.

Government of Canada, "Guidelines for the Negative Discretion Authority," online at https://www.canada.ca/en/immigration-refugees-citizenship/corporate/mandate/policies-operational-instructions-agreements/guidelines-negative-discretion-authority.html.

Gray, Mary W., "Universities in the West Bank and Gaza: An American professor revisits Palestine," *Academe* (May-June, 2013), online at https://www.aaup.org/article/universities-west-bank-and-gaza#.XZ3rAS2ZNMM.

Gross, Judah Ari, "Hamas Cell Planned Suicide and Car Bombings, Shin Bet Reveals," *The Times of Israel* (December 23, 2015), online at http://www.timesofisrael.com/hamas-cell-planned-suicide-and-car-bombings-shin-bet-reveals.

_____, "Shin Bet busts Hamas cell planning Jerusalem bombing attack," *The Times of Israel* (August 6, 2019), online at https://www.timesofisrael.com/shin-bet-busts-hamas-cell-planning-jerusalem-bombing-attack/.

Gunther, Inge, "Press freedom in Palestine: Condemned to self-censor," *Qantara.de* (August 28, 2017), online at https://en.qantara.de/content/gaza-and-the-west-bank-press-freedom-in-palestine-condemned-to-self-censor.

Hammond, Keith, "Palestinian Universities and the Israeli Occupation," *Policy Futures in Education* 5:2 (June 2007), 264-270.

Hanieh, Adam, "The End of a Political Fiction?" *The Bullet* (January 31, 2006), online at https://socialistproject.ca/2006/01/b13/.

Harel, Amos, and Amira Hass, "Twelve Suspected Collaborators Are Killed in W. Bank," *Haaretz* (April 2, 2002), online at https://www.haaretz.com/1.5278639.

Harel, Z., "Students Vs Administration: Crisis At Birzeit University In Palestinian Authority Following Ban On Military-Style Activity On Campus" *The MEMRI Daily* (January 15, 2020), online at https://www.memri.org/reports/students-vs-administration-crisis-birzeit-university-palestinian-authority-following-ban.

Hashweh, Maher, and Mazen Hashweh, and Sue Berryman, "An Assessment of Higher Education Needs in the West Bank and Gaza," United States Agency for International Development (September 2003), vii + 170 pp., online at https://pdf.usaid.gov/pdf_docs/Pnacw688.pdf.

Hass, Amira, "When a Haaretz Journalist Was Asked to Leave a Palestinian University," *Haaretz*, (September 28, 2014), online at http://www.haaretz.com/israel-news/.premium-1.618007.

_____, "Palestinian Authority Arrests More Than 100 Following Death of Jenin Governor," *Haaretz* (June 25, 2012).

Hassan, Budour Youssef, "Palestinian Authority Arrests Dissident Professor," *Electronic Intifada* (February 5, 2016), online at https://electronicintifada.net/content/palestinian-authority-arrests-dissident-professor/15526.

Heacock, Roger, "Birzeit and the International community." In Ida Audeh, ed. *Birzeit University: The Story of a National Institution*, pp. 73-77.

Herf, Jeffrey, "Historians Defeat Resolutions Denouncing Israel," *The American Interest* (January 10, 2020), online at https://www.the-american-interest.com/2020/01/10/historians-defeat-resolutions-denouncing-israel/.

Honour Based Violence Awareness Network, "Honor Killings on the Rise in West Bank; Palestinian Authority Calls for Culture Change" (22012), online at http://hbv-awareness.com/honor-killings-on-the-rise-in-west-bank-palestinian-authority-calls-for-culture-change/.

Horovitz, David, "Failed by Israel, Malki Roth's parents hope US can extradite her gloating killer," *Times of Israel* (May 5, 2020), online at https://www.timesofisrael.com/failed-by-israel-malki-roths-parents-hope-us-can-extradite-her-gloating-killer/.

Hoyle, Charlie, "Hamas executions in Gaza war designed to 'punish, instill fear,'" *Ma'an News Agency* (August 6, 2015), online at https://www.maannews.com/Content.aspx?id=765632.

Human Rights Watch, "Two Authorities, One Way, Zero Dissent: Arbitrary Arrest and Torture Under the Palestinian Authority and Hamas" (October 2018), online at https://www.hrw.org/report/2018/10/23/two-authorities-one-way-zero-dissent/arbitrary-arrest-and-torture-under.

Huus, Kari, "Hamas Bans Gaza Students Studying Abroad," *NBCnews.com* (August 17, 2011), online at http://www.nbcnews.com/id/44179843/ns/world_news-mideast_n_africa/t/hamas-bans-gaza-students-studying-abroad/#.V-VuRBSDeLs.

i24 News International, "Abbas and Dahlan supporters clash at Al Aqsa University" (April 16, 2018), online at https://www.i24news.tv/en/news/international/172463-180416-abbas-and-dahlan-supporters-clash-at-al-aqsa-university.

IMEMC News, "Abbas' Security Forces Assault Student from Al-Najah University" (April 9, 2019), online at https://imemc.org/article/abbas-security-forces-assault-student-from-al-najah-university/.

IMRA (Independent Media Review Analysis), "The suicide bombers and martyr culture at Al-Najah University in Nablus" (November 28, 2004), online at https://www.imra.org.il/story.php?id=22970.

Intelligence and Terrorism Information Center at the Center for Special Studies (C.S.S). *Suicide bombing terrorism during the current Israeli-Palestinian confrontation: September 2000–December 2005* (2006), online at https://www.terrorism info.org.il/Data/pdf/PDF_19279_2.pdf.

IOSAC, "Jerusalem 2016 Crime & Safety Report: Jerusalem, West Bank, and the Gaza Strip," U.S. Department of State: 2016, online at https://www.osac.gov/pages/ContentReportDetails.aspx?cid=19191.

Israel Defense Forces, "Hamas Indoctrinates Palestinian Youth After Kidnapping" (June 22, 2014), online at https://www.idf.il/en/articles/hamas/hamas-indoctrinates-palestinian-youth-after-kidnapping/.

Israel Security Agency, "Judea and Samaria Palestinian Students' Involvement in Terrorism," online at https://www.shabak.gov.il/SiteCollectionImages/english/TerrorInfo/studentsterror210709_en.pdf.

Issacharoff, Avi, "Israel foiled 17 suicide attacks so far this year, Shin Bet says," *The Times of Israel* (August 12, 2015), online at https://www.timesofisrael.com/israel-thwarted-17-suicide-attacks-so-far-this-year-shin-bet-says/.

_____, "What If the Hamas Terror Cell in Abu Dis Had Succeeded?" *The Times of Israel* (December 23, 2015), online at http://www.timesofisrael.com/what-if-the-hamas-terror-cell-in-abu-dis-had-succeeded/.

Jaschik, Scott, "Superman and Academic Freedom," *Inside Higher Education* (July 12, 2002), online at https://www.insidehighered.com/news/2012/07/05/did-birzeit-university-fail-protect-professor.

Jawabreh, Asma', "Palestinian Political Divisions Play Out at Birzeit University," *Al-Fanar Media* (November 12, 2015), online at http://www.al-fanarmedia.org/2015/11/palestinian-political-divisions-play-out-at-birzeit-university/.

Jensen, Michael Irving. *The Political Ideology of Hamas: A Grassroots Perspective.* London: I. B. Tauris, 2009.

JNS (Jewish News Syndicate), "Resolution to boycott Israeli academic institutions thwarted at annual poli-sci conference" (April 13, 2019), online at https://www.jns.org/resolution-to-boycott-israeli-academic-institutions-thwarted-at-annual-poli-sci-conference/.

_____, "Israel thwarts terror attack at Teddy Stadium in Jerusalem" (April 22, 2020), online at https://www.jns.org/israel-thwarts-terror-attack-at-teddy-stadium-in-jerusalem/.

Johnson, Penny, A—"Palestinian Universities Under Occupation," *Journal of Palestine Studies* 15:4 (Summer 1986), 127-33.

_____, B—"Palestinian Universities Under Occupation, June to August 1986," *Journal of Palestine Studies* 16:1 (Autumn 1986), 120-127.

_____, C—"Palestinian Universities Under Occupation, November 1986" *Journal of Palestine Studies* 16:2 (Winter 1987), 117-124.

_____, D—"Palestinian Universities Under Occupation, November 1986-January 1987," *Journal of Palestine Studies* 16:3 (Spring 1987), 134-141).

_____, E—"Palestinian Universities Under Occupation, May–July 1987," *Journal of Palestine Studies* 17:1 (Autumn 1987), 129–135.

_____, F—"Palestinian Universities Under Occupation, August–October 1987," *Journal of Palestine Studies* 17:2 (Winter 1988), 143–150.

_____, G—"Palestinian Universities Under Occupation, November 1987–January 1988" *Journal of Palestine Studies* 17:3 (Spring 1988), 100–105.

_____, H—Palestinian Universities Under Occupation, February–May 1988" *Journal of Palestine Studies* 17:4 (Summer 1988), 116–122.

_____, I—"Palestinian Universities Under Occupation, 15 August–15 November" *Journal of Palestine Studies* 18:2 (Winter 1989), 92–100.

_____, "Protests, Prisoners, and Palestinian Studies: What Can a University Under Occupation Do?" In Juliet Millican, ed, *Universities and Conflict: The Role of Higher Education in Peacebuilding and Resistance*. London: Routledge, 2018, pp. 78–89.

Kalman, Matthew, "6 Faculty Members at a Palestinian University Are Arrested for Suspected Hamas Ties," *The Chronicle of Higher Education* (August 4, 2010), online at https://www.chronicle.com/article/6-Faculty-Members-at-a/123764.

_____, "Palestinians Visit Auschwitz in First Organized Visit," *Haaretz* (March 27, 2014), online at https://www.haaretz.com/palestinian-students-visit-auschwitz-1.5340334.

_____, "The Real Lesson of Amira Hass' Ejection from a Palestinian University," *Haaretz* (September 30, 2014), online at http://www.haaretz.com/blogs/outside-edge/.premium-1.618420.

Kaplan, Amy, "In Palestine, Occupational Hazards," *Chronicle of Higher Education* (November 7, 2010).

Karagedik, Ulvi, "The Jews and the Hadith: A Contemporary Attempt at a Hermeneutic Interpretation." In Ednan Aslan and Margaret Rausch, eds. *Jewish-Muslim Relations: Historical and Contemporary Interactions and Exchanges*. Wiesbaden, Germany: Springer, 2019, pp. 35–49.

Katz, Yaakov, "IAF bombs Islamic University's R&D labs," *The Jerusalem Post* (December 29, 2008), online at https://www.jpost.com/Israel/IAF-bombs-Islamic-Universitys-R-and-D-labs.

Kerstein, Benjamin, "Israeli Security Forces Bust West Bank Hamas Cell Planning Major Jerusalem Terror Attack," *The Algemeiner* (August 6, 2019), online at https://www.algemeiner.com/2019/08/06/israeli-security-forces-bust-west-bank-hamas-cell-planning-major-jerusalem-terror-attack/.

Khoury, Jack, "Jordan Joins Israel in Clamping Down on Palestinian Transit Visas," *Haaretz* (May 16, 2016), online at https://www.haaretz.com/israel-news/.premium.MAGAZINE-jordan-clamps-down-on-palestinian-transit-visas-1.5383654.

Koni, Aida, and Khalim Zainal and Pn. Maznah Ibrahim, "An Overview of the Palestinian Higher Education," *International Journal of Asian Social Science* (2012), 2322-2329.

_____, "An Assessment of the Services Quality of Palestine Higher Education," *International Education Studies* 6: 2 (2013), 33-48.

Kuttab, Eileen, "Reflections on Education as a Political Practice: The Institute of Women's Studies and the Role of Research as a Vehicle for Change in Birzeit University, Palestinian Territories." In Juliet Millican, ed, *Universities and Conflict: The Role of Higher Education in Peacebuilding and Resistance.* London: Routledge, 2017, pp.163-175.

Levitt, Matthew. *Hamas: Politics, Charity, and Terrorism in the Service of Jihad.* New Haven: Yale University Press, 2006.

_____, "Teaching Terror: How Hamas Radicalizes Palestinian Society," *The Washington Institute* (February 12, 2007).

Levy, Elior, and Roi Yanovsky, "The Terror Academy" *Ynet News* (April 20, 2016), online at https://www.ynetnews.com/articles/0,7340,L-4794123,00.html.

Lybarger, Loren D. *Identity and Religion in Palestine: The Struggle Between Islamism and Secularism in the Occupied Territories.* Princeton: Princeton University Press, 2007.

Ma'an News Agency, "PA Rejects Political Motive in Arrest of Dissident Palestinian Professor" (February 3, 2016), online at https://www.maannews.com/Content.aspx?id=770094.

Marcus, Itamar, Nan Jacques Zilberdik and Alona Burger, "Palestinian Authority Education: A Recipe for Hate and Terror," *Palestinian Media Watch* (2015), online at https://palwatch.org/STORAGE/special%20reports/PMW%20Comprehensive%20Report%20on%20PA%20Education%20July%202015.pdf.

Marks, Jonathan, "A Model Response to BDS," *Commentary* (January 7, 2020), online at https://www.commentarymagazine.com/jonathan-marks/a-model-response-to-bds/.

Marks, Joshua Robbin, "Concern Increases That North Sinai Security Situation Deteriorating," *The Media Line* (May 10, 2020), online at https://themedialine.org/by-region/concern-increases-that-north-sinai-security-situation-deteriorating/.

McGough, Roger. *Bad Bad Cats.* London: Puffin, 1997.

_____. *Collected Poems.* London: Penguin Books, 2004.

Meir Amit Intelligence and Terrorism Information Center, "Incitement to terrorism by the Hamas student association at Al-Najah University in Nablus" (March 5, 2015), online at https://www.terrorism-info.org.il//Data/articles/Art_20782/E_036_15_1370380938.pdf.

Melhem, Ahmad, "Hamas-Fatah bitter split plays out in West Bank universities," *Al-Monitor* (January 6, 2019), online at https://www.al-monitor.com/pulse/originals/2018/12/west-bank-university-hamas-students-security-clashes.html.

MESA/CAF (Middle East Studies Association, Committee on Academic Freedom), "Controversy over Birzeit University Professor Musa Budeiri Caricatures Placed on His Office Door" (July 2, 2012), online at https://mesana.org/advocacy/committee-on-academic-freedom/2012/07/02/controversy-over-birzeit-university-professor-musa-budeiri-caricatures-placed-on-his-office-door.

_____, "Israeli Arrests of Palestinian Students and Professors, Israeli Assaults on Palestinian Campuses" (January 22, 2019), online at https://mesana.org/advocacy/committee-on-academic-freedom/2019/01/22/israeli-arrests-of-palestinian-students-and-professors-israeli-assaults-on-palestinian-campuses.

_____, "Israel's recent kidnapping of Birzeit University Student" (March 13, 2018), online at https://mesana.org/advocacy/committee-on-academic-freedom/2018/03/13/israels-recent-kidnapping-of-birzeit-university-student.

Middle East Monitor, "PA security officers shoot at Birzeit University students," (September 16, 2019), online at https://www.middleeastmonitor.com/20190916-pa-security-officers-shoot-at-birzeit-university-students/.

Military Wikia, "Hebrew University Bombing," online at https://military.wikia.org/wiki/Hebrew_University_bombing.

Miller, Elhana, "Hamas said to kill over 30 suspected collaborators with Israel," *The Times of Israel* (July 28, 2014), online at https://www.timesofisrael.com/hamas-said-to-kill-over-30-suspected-collaborators-with-israel/.

Miskin, Maayana, "Terrorist Killer Gets Life" *Arutz Sheva* (June 6, 2010), online at http://www.israelnationalnews.com/News/News.aspx/137914.

Murphy, John, "Palestinian University owes much to Hamas," *The Baltimore Sun* (February 12, 2006), online at https://www.baltimoresun.com/news/bs-xpm-2006-02-12-0602120105-story.html.

Myre, Greg, "Palestinian Universities Dragged Into Factional Clashes," *New York Times* (February 23, 2007), online at https://www.nytimes.com/2007/02/23/world/middleeast/23gaza.html.

Nelson, Cary. *Israel Denial: Anti-Zionism, Anti-Semitism, & the Faculty Campaign Against The Jewish State*. Bloomington: Indiana University Press/ Academic Engagement Network, 2019.

Nelson, Cary, and Gabriel Noah Brahm, eds. *The Case Against Academic Boycotts of Israel*. New York and Detroit: MLA Members for Scholars Rights/ Wayne State University Press, 2015.

Newman, Marcy, "Interview with PA Dissident: 'I cannot just stay silent,'" *Electronic Intifada* (November 26, 2009), online at https://electronicintifada. net/content/interview-pa-dissident-i-cannot-just-stay-silent/8551.

NGO Monitor, "Al-Haq" (February 19, 2020), online at https://www.ngo-monitor.org/ngos/al_haq/.

Nurding, Sam, "Al-Wasatia: Reviving the Palestinian Peace Camp: an interview with Professor Mohammed Dajani Daoudi," *Fathom* (February 2020), online at https://fathomjournal.org/al-wasatia-reviving-the-palestinian-peace-camp-an-interview-with-professor-mohammed-s-dajani-daoudi/.

Nusseibeh, Sari, with Anthony David. *Once Upon A Country: A Palestinian Life*. NY: Farrar, Strauss and Giroux, 2007.

Palestinian Center For Education and Cultural Exchange, "Honor Killing in Palestine" ((2018), online at https://gopalestine.org/honor-killing-in-palestine/.

Palestinian Centre for Human Rights, "PCHR Calls for Immediate Release of Dr. Abdul Satar Qassem" (February 7, 2016), online at http://pchrgaza. org/en/?p=7840.

Palestinian Journeys, "Gabi Baramki" (The Palestinian Museum and the Institute for Palestine Studies), online at https://www.paljourneys.org/en/ biography/14295/gabi-baramki.

Palestinian Media Watch, "Exhibit honoring Martyrs at USAID-funded Palestinian university glorifies bus bombings" (March 30, 2014), online at https://palwatch.org/page/6098.

Parry, Nigel. *Making Education Illegal: Students from the Gaza Strip—Israeli Restrictions and International Reactions*. Birzeit: Birzeit University Human Rights Action Project, 1995.

PCHR (Palestinian Centre for Human Rights), "PCHR Condemns Student Clashes in Al-Azhar University Yesterday" (May 5, 2008), online at https:// pchrgaza.org/en/?p=2682.

Rasgon, Adam, "Hamas court sentences 6 to death for 'collaborating' with Israel," *The Times of Israel* (December 3, 2018), online at https://www. timesofisrael.com/hamas-court-sentences-6-to-death-for-collaborating-with-israel/.

Redden, Elizabeth, "No Passage to Palestinian Universities," *Inside Higher Education* (July 26, 2019), online at https://www.insidehighered.com/news/2019/07/26/groups-protest-israeli-visa-policies-foreign-academics-teaching-west-bank.

Rense, "Hamas Offers Online 'Academy' How To Make Bombs." (Special to World Tribune—March 10, 2002), online at rense.com/general30/sdse.htm.

Riemer, Nick, "The Attack on Palestinian Universities," *Jacobin* (December 30, 2018), online at https://www.jacobinmag.com/2018/12/palestinian-universities-higher-eduction-israeli-violence.

Roberts, Adam, and Boel Joergensen and Frank Newman. *Academic Freedom Under Israeli Military Occupation: Report of WUS/ICJ Mission of Enquiry into Higher Education in the West Bank and Gaza.* London and Geneva: World University Service (UK) and International Commission of Jurists, 1984.

Robinson, David. *The Status of Higher Education Teaching Personnel in Israel, the West Bank and Gaza* (Ottawa: Canadian Association of University Teachers, 2010), online at https://download.ei-ie.org/Docs/WebDepot/The%20Status%20of%20Higher%20Education%20Teaching%20Personnel%20in%20Israel,%20the%20West%20Bank%20and%20Gaza.pdf.

Rossman-Benjamin, Tammi, "Identity Politics, the Pursuit of Social Justice, and the Rise of Campus Antisemitism: A Case Study." In Alvin H. Rosenfeld, ed. *Resurgent Antisemitism: Global Perspectives.* Bloomington, IN: Indiana University Press, 2013, pp. 482-520.

Roy, Sara. *Hamas and Civil Society: Engaging the Islamist Social Sector.* Princeton: Princeton University Press, 2011.

Salaita, Steven. I*nter/Nationalism: Decolonizing Native America and Palestine.* Minneapolis: University of Minnesota Press, 2016.

Schneider, Victoria, "In Gaza, authorities crack down on freedom of speech," *The New Arab* (November 13, 2017).

Scholars at Risk, "Free to Think: Report of the Scholars at Risk Academic Freedom Monitoring Project," New York, 2015, online at https://www.right-to-education.org/sites/right-to-education.org/files/resource-attachments/SAR%20Free%20to%20Think.pdf.

_____, "Free to Think 2016: Report of the Scholars at Risk Academic Freedom Monitoring Project," New York, 2016, online at https://www.scholarsatrisk.org/wp-content/uploads/2016/11/Free_to_Think_2016.pdf.

_____, "Free to Think 2017: Report of the Scholars at Risk Academic Freedom Monitoring Project," New York, 2017, online at https://www.scholarsatrisk.org/wp-content/uploads/2017/09/Free-to-Think-2017.pdf.

_____, "Free to Think 2018: Report of the Scholars at Risk Academic Freedom Monitoring Project," New York, 2018, online at https://www.scholarsatrisk.org/wp-content/uploads/2018/10/Free-to-Think-2018.pdf.

_____, "Free to Think 2019: Report of the Scholars at Risk Academic Freedom Monitoring Project," New York, 2019, online at https://www.scholarsatrisk.org/2019/11/free-to-think-2019-distressing-phenomenon-of-attacks-on-higher-education-demands-global-action/.

Shaked, Ronny, "Fatah: Shalit was held at Gaza Islamic University," *Ynet News* (June 2, 2007), online at https://www.ynetnews.com/articles/0,7340,L-3361595,00.html.

Shehada, Raja. *Occupier's Law: Israel and the West Bank.* Revised edition. Washington, DC: Institute for Palestine Studies, 1988.

Sneineh, Mustafa Abu, and Chloé Benoist, "Birzeit: How Palestinian students became the next generation of resistance," Middle East Eye (April 22, 2018), online at https://www.middleeasteye.net/news/birzeit-how-palestinian-students-became-next-generation-resistance.

Stein, Rebecca, "How One Palestinian University is Remaking 'Israel Studies,'" Middle East Research and Information Project (May 16, 2019), online at https://merip.org/2019/05/how-one-palestinian-university-is-remaking-israel-studies/. Reprinted on May 18, 2019, at https://www.birzeit.edu/en/blogs/how-one-palestinian-university-remaking-israel-studies, then by Mondoweiss on May 23, 2019.

Stillwell, Cinnamon, "Research on Terrorism and Extremism at An-Najah University," Campus Watch (September 15, 2016), online at https://www.meforum.org/campus-watch/24184/research-on-terrorism-and-extremism-at-an-najah.

Sullivan, Antony Thrall. *Thomas-Robert Bugeaud—France and Algeria, 1784-1849: Politics, Power, and the Good Society.* Hamden, CT: Archon Books, 1983.

_____. *Palestinian Universities Under Occupation.* Cairo, Egypt: The American University in Cairo Press, 1988.

_____, "Politics and Relevance in Palestinian Higher Education: The Case of Birzeit University," *American-Arab Affairs* XXVII (Winter 1988-89), 58-69.

_____, "Palestinian Universities in the West Bank and Gaza Strip," *Minerva* 29:3 (September 1991), 249-268.

_____, "Palestinian Universities in the West Bank and Gaza Strip" (revised), *The Muslim World* 84: 1-2 (January-April, 1994), 168-188.

Sweileh, Waleed M., and Sa'ed H. Zyoud, Suleiman Al-Khalil, Samah W. Al-Jabi, and Ansam F. Sawalha, "Assessing the Scientific Research Productivity of the Palestinian Higher Education Institutions: A Case Study at An-Najah National University, Palestine," SAGE Open 4:3 (2014), 1-11.

Tamimi, Azzam. H*amas: A History From Within*. Northhampton, MA: Olive Branch Press, 2007.

Taraki, Lisa, "The Development of Political Consciousness Among Palestinians in the Occupied Territories, 1967-1987." In Jamal R. Nassar and Roger Heacock, eds. *Intifada: Palestine at the Crossroads*. Birzeit, Palestine & NY: Birzeit University & Praeger, 1991, pp. 53-71.

Tawil, Bassam, "Palestinian Authority Silences Students" (July 25, 2018), *Gatestone Institute*, online at https://www.gatestoneinstitute.org/12753/palestinian-authority-silences-students.

Tayeh, Raced N., "Jailed Professor Talks About Palestinian Authority's Intolerance of Criticism," *Washington Report on Middle East Affairs* (April 2000), online at http://www.wrmea.org/2000-april/jailed-professor-talks-about-palestinian-authority-s-intolerance-of-criticism.html.

Toameh, Khaled Abu, "Palestinian Forces Arrest Professor Accused of Calling for Abbas Execution," *The Jerusalem Post* (February 2, 2016), online at http://www.jpost.com/Middle-East/Palestinian-forces-arrest-professor-accused-of-calling-for-Abbas-execution-44363.

_____, "Palestinians: Arbitrary Arrests, Administrative Detentions and World Silence," *Gatestone Institute* (February 2, 2018), online at https://www.gatestoneinstitute.org/11822/palestinians-arrests-detention.

_____, "Hamas police violently suppress Gaza student protest," *The Times of Israel* (March 26, 2018), online at https://www.timesofisrael.com/hamas-police-violently-suppress-gaza-student-protest/.

_____, "Palestinian Authority Targets Students," *Gatestone Institute* (April 9, 2019), online at https://www.gatestoneinstitute.org/14041/palestinians-target-students.

_____, "Palestinian university produces model for inexpensive respirator," *The Jerusalem Post* (April 5, 2020), online at https://www.jpost.com/middle-east/palestinian-university-produces-model-for-inexpensive-respirator-623251.

_____, "A Black Day for Palestinian Journalism" *Gatestone Institute* (May 20, 2020), online at https://www.gatestoneinstitute.org/16041/black-day-palestinian-journalism.

Visweswaran, Kamala, "Palestinian Universities and Everyday Life Under Occupation," *Academe* (September-October 2015).

Watt, Nicholas, "Danish paper sorry for Muhammad cartoons," *The Guardian* (January 31, 2006), online at https://www.theguardian.com/media/2006/jan/31/religion.saudiarabia.

Yeshiva World, The, "Arrests Made in Murder of Dr. Daniel Yaakobi" (June 17, 2009), online at https://www.theyeshivaworld.com/news/israel-news/35738/arrests-made-in-murder-of-dr-daniel-yaakobi.html.

Ynet News, "Fatah: Shalit was held at Gaza Islamic University" (June 2, 2007), online at https://www.ynetnews.com/articles/0,7340,L-3361595,00.html.

Zelkovitz, Ido. *Students and Resistance in Palestine: Books, guns and politics.* London: Routledge, 2015.

INDEX

Note, Figures and photographs are identified by italicized page numbers.

ABOUT THE AUTHOR

Cary Nelson is Jubilee Professor of Liberal Arts and Sciences and Professor of English at the University of Illinois at Urbana-Champaign and an Affiliated Professor at the University of Haifa. He is the recipient of an honorary doctorate from Ben-Gurion University of the Negev. His work is the subject of an edited collection, *Cary Nelson and the Struggle for the University: Poetry, Politics, and the Profession*. He was national president of the American Association of University Professors and is currently chair of the Alliance for Academic Freedom.

He is the author or editor of over thirty books and the author of 300 essays and reviews. Among his authored books are *The Incarnate Word: Literature as Verbal Space; Our Last First Poets: Vision and History in Contemporary American Poetry; Manifesto of a Tenured Radical; Revolutionary Memory: Recovering the Poetry of the American Left; No University is an Island: Saving Academic Freedom; Academic Keywords: A Devil's Dictionary for Higher Education* (with Stephen Watt); *Recommended Principles to Guide Academy-Industry Relationships* (with Jennifer Washburn); *Dreams Deferred: A Concise Guide to the Israeli-Palestinian Conflict & the Movement to Boycott Israel; and Israel Denial: Anti-Zionism, Anti-Semitism, & The Faculty Campaign Against the Jewish State*. His edited or coedited books include *Theory in the Classroom; Higher Education Under Fire; Marxism and the Interpretation of Culture; Cultural Studies; Madrid 1937: Letters of the Abraham Lincoln Brigade From the Spanish Civil War; Disciplinarity and Dissent in Cultural Studies; Will Teach for Food: Academic Labor in Crisis; The Wound and the Dream: Sixty Years of American Poetry About the Spanish Civil War; Anthology of Modern American Poetry;* and *The Case Against Academic Boycotts of Israel. Peace and Faith: Christian Churches and the Israeli-Palestinian Conflict* is forthcoming.

ABOUT AEN

Founded in 2015, the Academic Engagement Network (AEN) is a national organization of faculty members and staff on American university and college campuses which seeks to oppose efforts to delegitimize Israel, to support robust discussion, research, and education about Israel in the academy, to promote campus free expression and academic freedom, and to counter antisemitism when it occurs on campus.

In recent years, Israel's detractors on campus—both faculty and students—have used increasingly aggressive tactics to delegitimize Israel and demoralize its supporters. These have included attempts to exclude Jewish and Zionist students from participation in progressive coalitions, efforts to withdraw their own universities from study abroad and exchange relationships with Israeli academic institutions, campaigns seeking to discredit major Jewish American organizations and initiatives, denials of funding and recognition to pro-Israel student organizations, and refusals to write letters of recommendation for students wishing to study at Israeli universities. These currents result in a coarsened, hostile climate for Jewish and Zionist faculty and students and run contrary to the fundamental values of the academy.

AEN believes that faculty can play a critical role in countering these trends, including by using their institutional knowledge, authority, and academic expertise to speak, write, mentor students, host campus programs, work constructively with campus leaders and stakeholders, and more. To support members in their efforts to further the organization's goals, AEN provides micro-grants and other forms of financial support to faculty members to host campus programs; prepares guides and other educational resources; sponsors conferences, seminars, and convenings for faculty; offers advice and guidance to faculty members who are facing issues on their campuses; and connects and mobilizes members in a growing national multidirectional network.